HEROic Leadership

The Secret to Developing Stronger High Performing
Teams Using Psychological Capital

by Melonie Boone, Ph.D.

PRAISE FOR HEROic LEADERSHIP

"HEROic Leadership is a thought-provoking read for people leaders and HR professionals. Dr. Boone takes an innovative approach to positive psychology that will be an essential tool for you and your team; it will revolutionize how you build your team and utilize your team."

Erie S. Crawford, Ph.D., LSW, Founder, ESC Consulting, LLC

"So many of us define our paths forward in terms of the obstacles that block us. HEROic Leadership, instead, is about being optimistic that there is a way to achieve your goal, that obstacles are there to be overcome through resilience, and that doing so will make you effective in your work. At the core of this is hope, an under-appreciated building block of successful leadership. Hope is infectious, especially to your team members, and is the key motivator to action."

Paul Luongo, Chief Legal Counsel, SymphonyAI

"Dr. Boone has a unique gift for simplifying intricate data into comprehensible components. Through incorporating her personal anecdotes into the text, readers experience a lesson rather than a lecture. Her work not only captivates the audience but compels them to learn more. If you truly want to learn how to evolve and grow your organization into a more emotionally healthy and productive environment, you have to read this book."

Charita Lucas, Co-Founder, dOSA Naturals & Future Cycle Breakers

"HEROic Leadership is the perfect combination of being grounded in research and applicable in practical, pragmatic ways. It is an excellent guide for anyone currently managing people or aspiring to do so, that turns traditional man agreement philosophies completely upside down. Perhaps the best thing about this model is that it is grounded in Dr.Boone's beautiful relationship with her truly heroic mother!"

Vanessa Ruda, Ph.D., Senior Partner RHR International & Business Faculty at Northwestern University

"In a critical time for leadership, Dr. Boone provides a clear guidebook every leader needs to read. The world needs more HEROic Leadership".

Maria Malayter, Ph.D, Associate Professor of Business Psychology, The Chicago School of Professional Psychology

"The complexities of today's business environment leave many leaders in a state of indecision and inaction. Dr. Boone's HEROic concepts allow leaders to understand clearly how they can navigate, make decisions, and positively impact their organizations."

Tom Wimberly, Principal Consultant, Growth Mode Product Management Consulting

"HEROic leadership by Dr. Boone is a must-read for anyone interested in further developing their leadership capabilities. The HERO model, which emphasizes the importance of hope, efficacy, resilience, and optimism, provides a powerful framework for cultivating the skills and qualities that are essential for effective leadership in today's complex and dynamic world."

Kelly Porter, Sr. Vice President of Supply Chain at Conagra Brands

"The HERO model is an excellent guide to being an effective leader and building strong teams in today's uncertain world. With conflict constantly in our society and dramatic and unexpected business disruptions becoming commonplace, a model based on hope, resilience and overcoming adversity is exactly what is needed to drive effective leadership. Impressively, the HERO model is based not only on high-quality research, but also on Dr. Boone's professional learnings and personal experiences. This is not just a theory — it is a proven script for leadership success."

Richard C. Gay, Founder and Producer, 5 Pack Entertainment, Media Executive, Former Partner, Booz Allen & Hamilton

Book Cover by Mia Moore
Interior Design by Mia Moore

1st edition 2023

B Ana Studios
MEDIA PUBLISHING & PRODUCTION

www.banastudios.com

DEDICATION

I dedicate this book to my mother,
Bessie Martin-McCarty, the best ever example of HERO and
my pillar of strength, guiding light, and fount of wisdom and
grace. Her hope, efficacy, resilience and optimism taught me to
dream big and don't stop until I make my dreams come true.

In Loving Memory

Bessie Martin-McCarty

September 19, 1949 – December 8, 2020

ACKNOWLEDGEMENTS

This book would not have been possible without all the love and support of those who have encouraged me in my professional endeavors. Thank you to my partner in everything, my dear husband Connie, and my beautiful children, Sal and Ana, for being with me through this journey. Thank you to Cynthia and December, who share the special memories of the greatest HERO ever, our mother. I love you all!

Thank you to my publishing partners, Yayra Tsikudo, my constant support, Mia Moore, for her creative contribution, and Karen Dix, whose help was instrumental in turning my research and thought leadership into this book. Together we have created something that can empower better leaders in the world.

Finally, thank you to you, the reader, for picking up this book. We know it will make a difference in your life, your leadership, and your team at work. May you become the most HEROic leader, You can be!

CONTENTS

INTRODUCTION

In summer of 2020, I completed my doctoral dissertation to prove that positive leadership can have a positive effect on a team's job performance. I began my work on The *Impact of Leader Psychological Capital on Team Outcomes and Behaviors: A Multilevel Analysis* with the curiosity of a student and the experience of a veteran. For three years the journey engulfed my life with research, analysis, and documentation.

I was fascinated with the idea of the psychological leadership capital known as PsyCap and dreamed of adding to the body of knowledge on the subject already begun by other researchers such as Shu Ling Chen, James Avey, Bruce J Avolio, and Fred Luthans. They were able to empirically show that a follower who is (H)opeful, (E)fficacious, (R)esilient, and (O)ptimistic is more likely to be successful than followers with lower levels of PsyCap. These qualities, collectively known as HERO, made sense to me, even on a very personal level.

Why? For more than a decade as a speaker, coach, global executive, and consultant helping organization operations with strategy and human resources, people have remarked on my natural optimism and sunny nature. So, recognizing that I instinctively possessed some of these HERO qualities, I was determined to scientifically prove their effectiveness. While psychology traditionally focuses on what is wrong, positive psychology focuses on how to enhance what is working. I wanted to focus on the positive relationship between leaders with HERO (HEROic leaders) and their teams.

I developed several theories for my work. Alongside attempting to prove a positive relationship between a HEROic leader and their team, I also wanted to confirm a negative relationship between a leader with low HERO and their team's undesirable organizational behaviors. I further hypothesized that a highly HEROic leader would have a positive relationship with team job performance.

My research began as the world shut down during the first COVID-19 pandemic year. Through challenges and setbacks, I managed to assemble 80 participants to take part in the study from a variety of industries. Out of necessity, my methods varied from those of Chen, Luthans, and my other research predecessors, as did my population. I was operating during unprecedented times, just as the landscape of the workplace was shifting from the office to our homes. Despite the added challenges, I persevered and finished my research. Then, I examined the results... and my heart sank.

My study did not support any of my three hypotheses! My research had failed to prove something so intrinsically true to me. Yet many other researchers had proven similar hypotheses, so I knew that I was still on to something. I still believe in the positive relationship between a HEROic leader and the follower's level of HERO. I have personally witnessed how an individual's HERO leads to better teamwork and improves team performance.

I successfully defended my dissertation and earned my Ph.D. in organizational leadership. Although I did not add to the existing body of knowledge on HERO as I had intended, I had learned so much that I wanted to share the merits of HERO with others. I believe HEROic leadership and its ability to be assessed and developed, is a well-kept secret in the workplace today. Through this book, I hope to break open the importance of these competencies and reveal how they can be the key to the evolution and growth of any organization.

I write this book for people leaders and HR professionals, as well as anyone who works with others on a team. It's time we all understood the secret of HERO and how becoming a more HEROic leader is a critical path to a more emotionally healthy and productive workplace.

HERO is more than a set of four qualities; it is a blueprint for a more successful organization. PsyCap is the engine to fuel a more HEROic way of motivating and fortifying your team. I'm excited to let this secret out into the world. May this book create believers in the workplace! After all, the more HERO leaders we have out in the world, the more successful our world will be.

WHAT IS A HERO?

Chapter 1
What is a HERO?

My mother was my first hero. She was also my first HERO.

Bessie Martin-McCarty didn't know much about positive psychology or the HERO model of leadership. However, she still showed me that a little girl from southern Louisiana could be a powerful force in the world. As I grew up, she was always my positive motivation to be a good person and a true example of selflessness, giving, and always helping others. No matter how bad things got for her, we never felt it.

I grew up in the Hyde Park neighborhood of Chicago and south suburban University Park, the youngest of the three daughters in our family. My single mother had no more than a sixth-grade education, yet she owned a construction and a janitorial business. When I spent time helping clean buildings with her, she was actually teaching me a lesson about sweat equity and the entrepreneur.

My mom told us college was a requirement, not an option. She told us that if she had to clean buildings seven days a week, she was going to make sure all three of us went to college. I took her advice very seriously because I not only earned a bachelor's degree in human resource management from Loyola University but went on to earn an MBA, a Master of Jurisprudence (M.J.), and a Ph.D.!

I grew up and found a career in human resources. And whenever someone said to me, "Melonie, you're always so positive. How do you do it?" I always thought of my mother in gratitude. Ironically, my mom passed away in 2020, as I was in the middle of my research about positive leadership and HERO that she had personally inspired.

In a way, my mother was a leadership trendsetter, showing an example of positive leadership in an era where the opposite abounded. In her day (and at some companies today), worker well-being was not a major concern of most organizations. Now we see employee engagement as an important metric of organizational success (thank goodness!), but that was not always the case. And while many organizations are concerned with worker well-being, there is very little mention of positive psychology, PsyCap, or especially HERO in the workplace today. It is still just a well-kept secret.

The Road to PsyCap

When I took on my first HR role in 1996, I quickly noticed that the "human" element of my human resources department

[16]

was taking a backseat to our other activities. HR had "human" in the title, yet we did little to focus on people. We were "personnel" and more concerned about transactional tasks like payroll and cutting costs. Back then, "employee engagement" was not yet a conversation or even an industry buzzword. We were only aware that our managers had different leadership styles ranging from authoritative to laissez-faire.

Management was more about command and control in those days. Leaders gave orders, and their teams followed them. Historically I have always naturally rejected this leadership style. I have always tried to be a positive leader, to motivate and inspire my team, and lead with trust and transparency. As a result, I often butted heads with my managers. I would suggest solutions to alleviate a temporary pain with optimism about the outcome or the ability to adjust if necessary. I could see potential in an idea, and I envision a better way, even when management disagreed.

As I moved up in my career and began to lead HR functions, I developed my own leadership style. Little did I know that I was adopting PsyCap and the HEROic leadership model. Then when I finally discovered the concept of PsyCap and positive psychology during the orientation of my Ph.D. program, I felt like I had found a gas mask in a room full of toxic smoke. I started researching and learning more about positive psychology, and I realized how the approach closely aligned with my personal leadership style. I was so entranced with the topic that I rolled it into my doctoral dissertation and enjoyed every minute of the hard work it took to complete it.

First Came Positive Psychology

Historically, improving the workplace meant fixating on solving problems rather than introducing positive concepts. Then we saw the emergence of popular literature on workplace development, like *Who Moved My Cheese* by Spencer Johnson, *The One Minute Manager* by Kenneth Blanchard, and *Seven Habits of Highly Effective People* by Steven Covey. Such books were on the leading edge of positive literature, but were not evidence-based (Luthans, Youssef, et al., 2007). Still, they included self-reporting questionnaires, which may have provided some meaningful answers to their readers, but they needed more solid research to substantiate their predicted outcomes.

The field of Positive Organizational Behaviors (POBs) allows us to determine levels of positivity in the workplace, but in the late 1990's, the approach was in its infancy and had yet to grow and focus on positive state-like constructs. Positive Organizational Behavior, or POB, is "the study and application of positively oriented human resource strengths and psychological capacities that can be measured, developed and effectively managed for performance improvements in the workplace" (Luthans & Church, 2002 p. 59). POBs must meet four specific criteria to meet their standardized definition.

1. **They must first be positive**. Luthans argued that the early approaches to "fixing" rather than "enhancing" the workplace did more harm to performance, learning, and development than good

(Luthans, Youssef, et al., 2007) as POBs tried to focus on the untapped power of positivity and how it could contribute to the workplace (Luthans, Youssef, et al., 2007).

2. **They must be grounded in empirical research with valid measurements.** POBs must be state-like and amenable to development as well.

3. **They must have a quantifiable impact on performance.** POBs must ultimately show that they have a significant statistical effect on work outcomes (Luthans, Youssef, et al., 2007).

4. **Finally, POBs must have a psychological capacity**. Several positive psychological capacities were considered and studied to determine their impact on the workplace. Research determined that Hope, Efficacy, Resilience, and Optimism) best met the POB criteria (Jensen & Luthans, 2006; Luthans, 2002; Luthans, Vogelgesang, & Lester, 2006; Luthans & Youssef, 2004).

Another study examining the relationship between Authentic Leadership and positive organizational behaviors shows how important they are. The study notes that it could not analyze authentic leadership without including POB because it is challenging to study authentic leadership without understanding positive organizational behaviors (Yammarino et al., 2008). Thus, POB and criteria served as the foundation of what Luthans et al. termed Psychological Capital or PsyCap. Psychological capital "is a higher-order core construct that integrates the various POB criteria-meeting capacities...synergistically" (Luthans, Youssef, et al., 2007 p. 19) PsyCap is a second-order factor that measures a person's motivational ability as a result of their psychological resources, mainly Hope, Efficacy, Resilience, and Optimism (Luthans, Avolio, et al., 2007).

PsyCap is a relatively young construct compared to other organizational and leadership theories. The earliest mentions were by notable researchers like Fred Luthans, Carolyn Yousef, Bruce Avolio, and James Avey in the early 2000s. The wonderful thing about PsyCap is that it is state-like, meaning it is open to development and change (Luthans, Avolio, et al., 2007). In fact, studies show that PsyCap interventions, which are meant to improve an individual level of PsyCap, result in improving an individual's performance (Luthans et al., 2010).

Fred Luthans is considered a father of organizational behavior and pioneered the study of positive psychology in the workplace. He took the idea of positive leadership one step further with his colleagues and developed a leadership model encapsulating a positive leader's main characteristics. Today this model is known as HERO. The acronym stands for Hope, Efficacy, Resilience, and Optimism.

PsyCap in the Workplace

At first glance, the four words that comprise the acronym, HERO, are not the typical characteristics that supervisors evaluate in their employee review sessions. We would be hard-pressed to find someone who was promoted for being optimistic or given a raise for being hopeful. However, HERO is not only helpful for the emotional health and personal growth of leaders; it creates better employees.

Research proves it.

Positive psychology has been linked to desirable employee attitudes and behaviors. (J. B. Avey et al., 2011). There is an increasing amount of evidence about the value of having a positive mindset. The same has been validated concerning positive approaches in the workplace (J. B. Avey et al., 2011). The state of mind that guides behavior and envelops HERO is known as psychological capital, or PsyCap.

PsyCap has been studied extensively. Positive PsyCap was shown to have a positive relationship with employee empowerment and an even stronger predictor than transformational leadership, which is explicitly focused on change. (J. B. Avey et al., 2008). When leaders draw from positive PsyCap, they promote similar positive states in others (Rego, Filipa, Maques, & Cunah, 2012, p, 432), specifically those who report to them. High levels of PsyCap were also found to increase employee creativity (Rego, Filipa, Maques, & Cunah, 2012, p. 435), boost employees' morale, lower employee turnover intentions, increase job satisfaction, and increase psychological well-being at work (Avey, Reichard, Luthans, & Mhatre, 2011, p. 146). Leaders can use PsyCap to enhance workplace programs such as stress management, wellness programs, and onboarding for new hires. Imagine if you could increase your level of PsyCap. Do you think you would be happier and more productive?

It's indisputable that the level of a leader's PsyCap directly affects their team members. Managers with high PsyCap generally have direct reports with high PsyCap. You can spot a leader or team member with higher PsyCap by their demonstrated "organizational citizenship behaviors" or OCBs. These are actions that employees willingly do but are not part of their formal job description. They are actions that support the entire organization, not simply the employee. An example might be covering responsibilities for a colleague when they are sick or cleaning up a common work area without being asked.

Conversely, employees with low PsyCap demonstrate behaviors that are primarily counterproductive or undesirable in the workplace (Avey, Reichard, Luthans, & Mhatre, 2011, p 133). They may complain, or be uncooperative and self-focused, with no regard for the common good of the organization.

The good news is that Luthan's research has shown that PsyCap can grow in individuals and, consequently, in teams. (Luthans, 2012). The results from his study alone (although there are many others) indicate that HERO is an area that can be nurtured and cultivated within the workplace for measurable increases in worker performance.

Imagine if the development of HERO could find its way into your organization as part of their routine internal leadership training. Again, HERO is a secret sitting in broad daylight for organizations to put into action. The results could be staggering.

PsyCap's Vehicle: HERO

Hope, Efficacy, Resilience, and Optimism are the critical resources leaders must have to be considered HEROic. I have never been in an organization or been evaluated by a manager based on my levels of "hope" or my "resilience" on the job. However, I know from monitoring myself that when I feel the levels of HERO climb within me, I feel happier and accomplish more at work.

***Hope* is the expectation or desire for a certain thing to happen.**

When we think about the word hope, we usually think about our desires. It is safe to say that everyone has something they want or hope to get. The educational definition of *hope,* in the context of PsyCap, is defined by Luthans and Jensen:

> "...A bi-dimensional construct composed of both agency (a sense of willpower, or determination to begin and maintain the effort needed to achieve goals) and pathways (a sense of waypower or belief in one's ability to generate successful plans and alternatives when obstacles are met in order to meet desired goals)."

Hope is state-like, which means it is open to development. A hopeful individual sets challenging goals and expectations that are realistic. They achieve their goals through self-directed initiative, energy, and determination (Luthans, Youssef, et al., 2007). In other words, the hopeful leader wants something and has the persistence to get it.

Hopeful leaders are not unrealistic. They recognize when things are not going as planned. However, the difference between the hopeful leader and the one lacking hope is that the hopeful leader is confident that if things don't go well, they will be able to fix them.

I once consulted with a CEO (we'll call him Adam) whose company was going through a very rough time. He worked in an industry hit hard by the pandemic, and along with other painful issues, the company was looking at an income loss for the first time in thirty years. However, Adam's high amount of PsyCap allowed him to stay positive and encourage his team. He rallied them to persevere and shared his hope by metaphorically helping them imagine the light at the end of the tunnel that he believed was inevitable. He was there, working nights and weekends alongside the team, showing his commitment to the project. Had he revealed the frustration and fear he felt to his team, he undoubtedly would have shaken everyone. Instead, his hope reassured the team that everything would be ok.

Efficacy is defined as the belief or judgment that someone can succeed.

The second resource in the HERO acronym is "E" for efficacy. In our culture, we define efficacy as the ability to create a desired effect. For example, drug companies are concerned with the efficacy of their drugs. However, efficacy, as defined by researchers Sable, Larrivee, & Gayer, is "...the belief or judgment made by an individual that they can succeed or accomplish an identified task." (Sable, Larrivee, & Gayer, 2008)

Often referred to as confidence or self-esteem, efficacy centers around a person's belief in their ability to complete a task or meet a goal. The most notable behavioral psychologist who helped define self-efficacy was Albert Bandura. (Sable et al., 2008). Bandura's work on self-efficacy began in 1977 and spanned over twenty years. It resulted in the concept of efficacy within specific situations where we must make judgments about our ability to complete a task (Sable et al., 2008). As a resource to PsyCap, self-efficacy is considered a measure of someone's ability to take on a task and their willingness to put in the necessary work to complete it (Larson & Luthans, 2007).

Like other resources, self-efficacy can be developed. In at least one study, findings show that leaders can improve follower self-efficacy by sharing personal experiences. For example, if a manager shares an experience of how they overcame their fear of public speaking with a team member, it may give that team member more confidence to make a speech. This kind of sharing can be an essential resource that positively impacts job performance (Chen, 2015).

Leaders with self-efficacy are self-motivated, believe in their abilities, and do not need outside validation. If they do not know how to do something, they are confident they will figure it out. Conversely, leaders lacking self-efficacy doubt themselves and need validation that they are on the right track. Their fear of failure is stronger than their belief in their ability to complete the task.

Resilience is how we adjust to change.

When people speak of others as being "resilient," they often refer to how an individual overcame a misfortune or traumatic event. However, within HERO, the definition is broader:

"The developable capacity to rebound or bounce back from adversity, conflict, failure or even positive events, progress, and increased responsibility." *(Luthans, 2002)*

Few people would call receiving a promotion at work a negative event. Yet individuals with low resilience will have a more difficult time adjusting to their new work role than those with high levels of resilience. Resilience is indeed one's ability to "bounce back" from any change, whether positive or negative.

In PsyCap research, Resilience was initially thought to be a hard-to-find personality trait (Luthans et al.,2006) until a study on schizophrenic mothers and their children (Garmezy, 1971, 1974; Masten, Best, & Garmezy, 1990) found that resilience is more common than previously thought. (Luthans et al., 2006). Like the other resources of PsyCap, it can be developed (Luthans et al., 2007). Resilience as a resource to PsyCap was studied by Amy Masten (2001), a positive psychologist focused on the positive approach to assessing risks and assets that can affect an employee (Luthans et al., 2006). She found that resilience is not merely reactive; it can be proactive and grow as an individual experiences various situations in life (Youssef & Luthans, 2007a).

Resilient people always have a conscious or subconscious plan to adapt to new circumstances. They implement the plan and keep going. For example, the first time they found a tumor in my mother's brain, she went to surgery, did her rehab, and returned to work. She kept going by living her life in a new way. She did it again after they found a second tumor. Her resilience was one of her greatest strengths. She modeled it well and passed it on to her daughter.

The final resource creating the HERO construct is Optimism.

Optimism is looking at events in a positive way.

The world brands people as "optimists" if they usually frame events in a positive way. The word is even used sarcastically for people who see things as positive when all hope is lost. Researchers of PsyCap define it this way:

> "a positive explanatory style that attributes positive events to personal, permanent, and pervasive causes, and interprets negative events in terms of external, temporary, and situation-specific factors." (Luthans & Youssef-Morgan, 2017)

Optimism is also a positive state-like construct to be developed. Optimistic people assign positive events to experiences and view adverse events as temporary and situation-specific (Luthans & Youssef-Morgan, 2017). An optimistic person believes there will be a positive outcome even in the most stressful, seemingly doomed situations. In other words, optimistic individuals expect success (J. B. Avey et al., 2008).

Being HEROic

As you can see, having high levels of PsyCap in all four resources within the HERO construct is the secret to becoming a mighty, compelling leader! In fact, the best word to describe them would be as a HEROic leader.

Pulling from positive psychology, Youssef and Luthans found a significant positive correlation between performance, hope, optimism, and resilience. They showed that the core tenants of PsyCap have a positive effect on individual behaviors and outcomes. Hope, Optimism, and Resilience share commonalities that support self-motivation and can have a desirable impact on attitudes at work and in job performance (Youssef & Luthans, 2007).

Within my research study, my review of others, and my experience as a coach and consultant, I am more convinced than ever of the need for PsyCap in the workplace to combat multiple challenges, from a growing remote workforce to a retiring generation and the rise of a new breed of worker. There is only one kind of leader who will be successful in this complex, changing order--the HEROic one!

Why Do We Need HEROic Leaders?

Chapter 2

Why do we need HEROic Leaders?

It's established that PsyCap is the key to becoming a HEROic leader (one with Hope, Efficacy, Resilience, and Optimism), and these qualities can be developed. The next question is, why should we take the time to develop them?

The answer is that the HEROic leader is needed more now than ever before in history!

From Survive to Thrive

In today's business climate, organizations are operating in volatile and uncertain times concerning expectations and the workforce. We know that many circumstances determine the health of a business. Some are beyond the CEO's control, such as the recent pandemic or a war in another country. Others are within their control, such as their labor force and management style. Employees, too, are doing their best to stay afloat. Where once remote work was unheard of, it is now a negotiating point for some employees to accept a position at a new company. And with the number of people in the workforce involved in "gig work" at an all-time high, freelancers and contractors are now treated like a branch of small businesses. Case in point: freelancers could apply for federal loan assistance alongside the other small businesses to float along during the pandemic.

It's clear that the workforce has evolved more rapidly since COVID-19 graced the world. Years earlier, Luthans prophetically wrote that the workplace is becoming a place where survival, let alone success, necessitates a higher-than-average performance (Luthans & Youssef, 2003). Many of us have seen this in our jobs. As more people leave the workforce, often the employees who remain are given even more responsibility (many times without a pay increase). At some organizations, expectations of work quality have increased as well. For example, where once an employee was expected to produce five reports a week, they may suddenly be expected to produce seven. New expectations put pressure on employees. However, managers are also squeezed to keep employees feeling motivated and supported in the company, even amid unpleasant circumstances.

In response, many organizations have changed their hiring practices. Today's organizations are more cognizant of the importance of hiring a diverse, global workforce. People managers must often meet the demands of their job while leading teams with cultural differences.

A famous study on culturally linked leadership styles by Uma D. Jogula found a difference in leadership styles based on cultural groups. The study suggests that perceptions of leadership vary depending on a person's cultural background (Jogulu, 2010). Jogula performed the study across middle managers from two cultural backgrounds (Malaysian and Australian) working within four similar industries. They found evidence to support the argument that culture, and leadership interact differently in diverse contexts. Through a multifactor leadership questionnaire and an analysis of the findings, the data showed that transactional leadership (which focuses on supervision, organization, and performance) strongly aligns with the ratings of managers from Malaysia. In Australia, transformational leadership scales (in which leaders work with employees beyond their immediate self-interests to identify change) correlate with the Australian respondents' mean ratings. Jogula concluded that the variations in leadership styles are due to cultural influences because people have different beliefs and assumptions about characteristics that are deemed appropriate for leadership. Therefore, to be more effective leaders, it is fundamental to know what skills and knowledge are valued most by managers and employees on a global level. (Jogula, 2010).

Organizations often find themselves overtaxed to meet varied demands and overcome constraints to ensure a highly engaged workforce. Meanwhile, they strive to cultivate environments that allow their employees to flourish and want to remain at the company.

Role Ambiguity in the Workplace

In addition to dealing with emerging societal conditions and diversity, people managers can also create additional problems. If they are not careful, people managers can inadvertently introduce environmental stressors into their organization. These stressors can adversely affect employees and create tension and negativity in the workplace. They can be remedied, but the first step is recognizing their existence. Some of the most common stressors are role ambiguity and role conflict.

It's amazing to think that many employees struggle to understand their role at their company. Most well-established companies have job descriptions for each of their positions, a complete description of responsibilities, and even metrics as to how the employee will be evaluated. However, I have also worked with billion-dollar companies without roles and responsibilities solidly in place. I discover this as I delve into the organization and find employees who have become disengaged or disillusioned with their work at the company. In some cases, they are not sure how their work impacts the organization, the customer, or society. In worst-case scenarios, their work duplicates their teammate's work. Some employees have told me they have been with the company for thirty years and have never had a performance review!

This kind of role ambiguity often infiltrates the culture of a company. People managers incorrectly begin to make assumptions that employees "just know what to do" when employees are more confused than ever. Typically, employees do what they *think* they are supposed to be doing. However, without clear direction and evaluation of reaching specific goals, an employee can feel adrift in an ocean of randomly created waves, bobbing untethered, without a stretch of land in sight. And when an employee feels confused, unappreciated, and disengaged at the company, resignation is surely just around the corner.

This "role ambiguity" is one of the enemies of a thriving workforce. Studies have shown that to not only survive but thrive in the workplace, roles must be clearly defined. Otherwise, there will be confusion among the team. In any department, team members should understand what everyone else is doing. They should never look at a co-worker running reports at their desk all day and wonder what they are doing or how they are contributing to the organization. They should know and understand the co-worker's role at the company, as well as their own!

Role Conflict in the Workplace

In one study, another important stressor, "role conflict," was also examined. Conflict can take the form of disagreement between an employee and another person (person-role conflict) or how they are perceived by others (sender-role conflict). The amount of role conflict that respondents in the survey experienced affected their outlook on the probability of their future employment. The study showed evidence that the existence of both role ambiguity and role conflict can be detrimental to job performance. (Abramis, p. 550)

However, while role ambiguity and role conflict can sink many employees, others can still thrive in such an environment. People with high "E" (Efficacy) will find out on their own what each team member is doing. They will then see what needs to be done and start on it. People without this self-efficacy will struggle; they need to be given specific tasks to do and be provided with all information and clearly outlined responsibilities in order to complete their work. If these people have a manager that is completely hands-off, their productivity will plummet. The team will have serious issues, and productivity will suffer dramatically.

Both role ambiguity and role conflict can negatively impact job performance (Abramis & Beach, 2017). In defense of management, however, it is evident that many leaders are ill-equipped to meet the demands of the current workplace. Yesterday's management rules do not always apply to today's employees because the workforce has evolved. Leaders can no longer operate as they have in the past. However, with the right set of competencies, people managers can significantly impact their teams.

Role ambiguity and conflict impact the various stakeholders of the company, including customers, employees, and partners, because they contribute to short-term performance failure in the workforce. Over the long term, if not addressed, role ambiguity and conflicts can adversely affect an organization's growth and even its ability to achieve lasting success. The consequences can be dire.

Additional Challenges

Other important factors, too, contribute to the problems within today's workforce. These include:

- **Outdated human resources development strategies.** Indeed, one of the reasons I am writing this book is to call attention to PsyCap as a positive tool to remedy outdated human resources strategies typically seen in today's business world. A HEROic model of training equips management to work with the changing workforce by developing people manager's competencies, as well as competencies within those they manage. It's a win-win for the leader and the employee.

- **Little to no leadership development among managers.** When it comes to leadership development, it is *quality,* not *quantity,* that matters. Yet I've worked with many companies who don't offer either, and it often shows in the productivity and happiness of their workforce. When the C-level fails to develop leadership skills in their managers, they fail to make an investment in the future of the company. In turn, they miss the opportunity to empower and engage their workforce through an even stronger and well-prepared manager.

- **Cultures that do not embrace or encourage change.** Sometimes, for several varied reasons, a company's culture is simply resistant to change. Perhaps the person at the top feels things are working fine the way they are and simply does not have a vision for change. Or someone else brings them a viable vision, but fear and doubt keep them from embracing it. Whether a company embraces change or not, the world will certainly keep changing. Therefore, upholding the status quo when a change would be prudent is one-way companies ultimately fail.

- **Lack of knowledge around emerging leadership methodologies.** As mentioned before, what worked yesterday for managing employees may not work today. As the workforce changes, so do employee expectations of their employers, especially regarding management style and company culture. If managers are adhering to the "command and control" model of leadership, which was popular twenty years ago, they may soon find disgruntled employees on their hands. Just as business changes with economic conditions, so a company's leadership style must adapt to changing societal and cultural forces.

PsyCap in the Ambiguous Workforce

Once again, we find that positive psychology and PsyCap can rescue a flailing corporate environment. PsyCap encapsulates the competencies that management needs to positively relate to desirable employee attitudes and behaviors in all areas of a people manager's responsibilities (J. B. Avey et al., 2011). The HEROic tendencies of Hope, Efficacy, Resilience, and Optimism are all geared toward producing happier, more productive employees. Therefore, it makes complete sense that when PsyCap interventions are incorporated into a company's human resources development strategies, it is an opportunity for the company to gain a true competitive advantage.

The many issues faced by companies today are assuaged by PsyCap and the HEROic model of leadership. Let's imagine a HEROic team where each member possesses all four HERO competencies. With high levels of hope and optimism, the team could see beyond the company's current processes and envision something even better. They could imagine and develop an updated process without fear of change. A team with high self-efficacy would clearly define their roles and responsibilities, which would banish role conflict and ambiguity, keeping the team happy, focused, and productive. Finally, a highly resilient team would be able to respond to organizational change with agility and positivity. Could you imagine such a dream team at your company? The results would be remarkable!

Just as exciting is the research by Chen that found that leaders who have higher levels of psychological capital can transfer those high levels to their direct reports (Chen, 2015). His study was one of the few multi-level studies investigating the relationship between leader PsyCap and follower outcomes. However, it is still significant because it provided empirical evidence for the positive relationship between leader

PsyCap and follower performance and engagement. The bottom line is that leaders with high PsyCap positively impact their teams in both job performance and organizational citizenship behaviors (those actions that employees take outside of their job descriptions because they see it needs to be done). When a people manager models these organizational citizenship behaviors, as "Adam" did in Chapter 1, it's infectious. By stepping out of his managerial role and working alongside his people to get things done, he inspired others to work with similar dedication towards the common goal. It's evident that adopting PsyCap in a managerial model can have positive, significant results. However, there is another factor that affects how raising PsyCap in the workplace will manifest itself within your own organization's workforce. And it has to do with when your employees were born.

HEROic Generations

Chapter 3

HEROic Generations

We've established that being a people manager comes with a variety of challenges to overcome and that PsyCap can help do it. Leaders who are ill-equipped to meet the demands of business will find themselves stuck in a revolving door of employees and a static grind of status quo, even though problems at the company beg to be addressed. It all makes for a no-win scenario for the poor manager.

Further complicating the task is the makeup of today's workforce, which is, as it has always been, multigenerational. Perhaps the difference today, though, is the amount of disparity between the generations and the pressure to cultivate as well as competently lead this diverse workforce. People managers today are even tasked with delivering better, faster results from their multigenerational team, so it's important that they understand them and lead with as much preparation as possible.

There are currently five generations making up global teams today, according to the Center for Women and Business at Bentley University. These break down into 2% of Silent Generation workers (age 71-89), 29% of Baby Boomers (age 53-70), 34% Generation X workers (age 37-52), 34% Millennial workers (age 19-36) and 1% of Generation Z workers (age 0 – 18) (Various, 2017). Let's examine each one and how PsyCap is received through them.

The Silent Generation

If you have grandparents or elderly parents, they are most likely part of the "Silent Generation." These workers are categorized as born between the years 1928-1945. They have memories of World War II, and in many cases, it may have been part of their formative experience. Members of the Silent Generation were typically raised in disciplined, nuclear families and embrace a strong sense of loyalty to their member groups, including their workplace. They are team-centric, patriotic, and family-oriented. As some of them are "children of the Great Depression," they value the opportunity to work but still value flexibility in how, when, and where they work. (Various, 2017).

Silents are often known for respecting authority, avoiding risks, and following rules. Because of their age, this generation is rapidly disappearing from the workplace landscape. However, PsyCap is just as palpable for their development as the workers in the other various generations.

Baby Boomers

The number of Baby Boomers in the workforce has recently been in decline. Born between 1946-1964, this group is characterized by their hardworking nature. They often prioritize work over personal life. Their childhood was marked by the moon landing, the Civil rights movement, the Kennedy assassination, the Vietnam War, and the women's liberation movement. (Burtsh and Kelly)

Hit hard by the 2008 recession, this generation is also remaining in the workforce longer than expected. Job security is paramount to them. (Rodriguez, Five Strategies to Manage Generational Differences) As such, they are often more optimistic and open to change. (AMA)

Studies show what this generation appreciates when it comes to management:

- Phased retirement programs (AMA)
- Opportunities to mentor others (Moss)
- Opportunities to collaborate and interact in meetings (Notter)
- Recognition through compensation and promotion (Rodriguez)

Of the intergenerational working relationships, Boomers have the most trouble working with Millennials. In a survey, both parties reported the perception that the other dismissed their past experiences, lacked respect, or was unwilling to change or innovate (Burtsh and Kelly p. 12). There is also a difference in technological literacy between these two groups and a disparity about how best to send and receive information (oral or digitally). (Burtsh and Kelly p. 12).

Generation X

Currently, Generation X makes up the largest generation of workers in the workforce. As opposed to the Silent Generation, Generation Xers (born 1965-1980) are children of change. Formative life events include the energy crisis, Watergate, the AIDS epidemic, Chernobyl, and the fall of the Berlin Wall. (Bursch, D. and Kelly, K. *Managing the Multigenerational Workplace, 2014*) Gen Xers appear to be more independent and adaptable, probably because most were in the workforce during the rise of technology and were required to adapt. They are credited with creating the concept of work/life balance and are more likely to question authority at work. (AMA) This is partially because Gen Xers were raised with laxer parental supervision than their successors, the Millennials. (AMA, leading the four generations at work)

While more than a third of the workforce is within Generation X, the Baby Boomers are gaining on them. Gen Xers value opportunities that serve them in the long run over finding a job that will allow them to stay put. (Rodriguez) These are suggested ways to attract and retain Gen Xers:

- Avoid micromanagement (97)
- Give well-defined, measurable goals with timely feedback
- Be flexible about how and where work gets done

- Allow opportunities for new experiences, ongoing training, and skill development (99)

Millennials

Also known as Generation Y, Millennials comprise another large percentage of the workforce. Born between the years 1981-1998, they are considered the most educated and diverse generation. (15 & 16) They are also energetic, technically savvy, and socially conscious. This generation saw the Columbine shooting, 9/11, Enron, Hurricane Katrina, and the rise of the internet. (17)

As the Boomers retire, more Millennials will be transitioning from college and joining the workforce. After watching the Boomers work at the expense of their family, Millennials embrace work/life balance and the freedom to decide how they want to work. (30) They lead the generations in the desire for workplace flexibility and parental leave. Seventy-eight percent of them are likely to have a partner working full-time, as opposed to 47 % of Boomers. (32)

Millennials "work to live" (34) but like the Silent Generation, they are team-centric, patriotic, and family-oriented. They have an appreciation for diversity and inclusion and value a socially responsible workplace. (35) In fact, a 2016 Millennial Survey reported that 56 percent of Millennials ruled out working for a company based on the company's values. (36) This figure speaks to the Millennial's need to feel that their work is meaningful and more than a paycheck. (37).

Millennials have a reputation for changing jobs frequently, which leads others to believe they are disloyal. However, it speaks to how millennials are unwilling to make a job their top priority. (43) They view individual jobs as steps to personal growth, not destinations, and instead value professional development and career security over job security. (45) Millennials also share an unsubstantiated reputation for lacking motivation, yet a 2016 ManpowerGroup Report showed that Millennials work an average 45-hour work week and work as hard, if not harder, than other generations. (54)

Because Millennials were raised with close parental supervision, they crave constant feedback and praise. (48) They appreciate when their managers coach or mentor them and invest in their professional development. (52) They are also redefining diversity in the workplace by coming from more single-parent homes, blended families, and same-sex families than ever before. Thus, they value an inclusive workplace. (84)

Companies who actively try to attract and engage Millennials will try to do the following.

- Create a socially conscious workplace (88)
- Involve Millennials in a higher company mission (90)
- Provide flexibility for Millennials to innovate, change processes, develop new programs and take risks (91)

- Offer contingent work opportunities as you scale up and down (92)
- Offer frequent, face-to-face feedback, recognition, and affirmation (94 & 95)

Millennials bring their own strengths to the leadership arena and even the opportunity to reverse mentor older generations with their technological knowledge.

Generation Z

The final slice of the workforce that is tiny at present but poised for rapid growth is Generation Z, born after 1999. These workers grew up in a completely wireless world and never knew a time without smartphones and social media. (24) After watching their parents struggle financially during the 2008 recession, they are more entrepreneurial than other generations but also cautious and concerned with career stability (22&23). Brought up in an ecosystem of financial concern, with rising healthcare costs and mounting student debt, Gen Z is slightly more jaded and financially driven than the Millennials. (39) Still, they value work-life balance, and their constant digital interaction fuels their need for instant gratification. (67)

The Generations and PsyCap

As you strive to develop the resources of HERO with your team, consider the needs of each individual as well as the orientation of their generation. They will each have their challenges based on their experiences and the parenting style of their generation.

Gen Xers, who bring an adaptable mindset to the workplace, may be brimming with resilience and self-efficacy but challenged with hope and optimism. The Millennials, while idealistic and raised by more watchful parents, may need to develop greater self-efficacy through positive experiences and praise. They may also need to develop the resilience to pick up the pieces when things don't work out. The up-and-coming Generation Z was raised on a steady diet of internet exposure and possibly periods of financial insecurity. They may have a special need to develop their hope and optimism. As a manager, be aware of the generational differences as you plan your interventions but be open to the independent differences of each team member as well.

It's clear that the hot spot to watch in emerging leadership in the workplace lies between the aging Gen Xers and the emerging Millennials. As the Silent Generation and Baby Boomers are moving out of the workforce, companies are continuing to lose knowledge and experience. The Millennials are moving into leadership roles but often lack the skills to be successful. Meanwhile, Generation Xers often cling to outdated leadership styles as they step into executive leadership. Now more than ever, helping your team members develop all the HEROic resources within PsyCap can shape stronger leaders in Gen X and the rising leaders in the other generations too.

Being HEROic with HOPE

Chapter 4

Being HEROic with HOPE

If we think back to the first time we ever heard the word "hope," we would probably think of our childhood. Perhaps we hoped we would get a certain toy for Christmas or that our friend would be in the same elementary school class with us the following year. Back then, hope may have entailed simple wishes. In business, it is so much more. Hope refers to how we handle problems, especially when obstacles stand in the way of solutions.

Positive psychology researchers Luthans & Jensen defined hope as more than wishful thinking. The simple definition was "persevering towards goals and, when necessary, redirecting paths to goals (hope) in order to succeed." (Luthans F., 2007).

Hope, particularly as a construct in PsyCap, has been well studied. Psychologist C.R. Snyder is a pioneer in "hope theory" and one of the first to break hope down into three essential components. (Luthans & Jensen, 2002) His research showed that hope included:

1) **Goal setting**, to have an aim or objective to pursue.
2) The **willpower** to begin something and maintain the effort needed to achieve the goal.
3) The **waypower** to generate successful plans and alternatives, even when obstacles stand in the way.

It's exciting to think this high hopefulness is not just something we're born with. We can develop it! Positive psychologists have examined this construct for years to determine whether hopefulness is a static quality we are born with or a "state" that can be developed. Snyder described hope as an enduring mindset but also emphasized that it can be developed as well. He believed that although hope is potent in children, mature adults too can be open to a change in overall hope. (Snyder, C.R. Simpson, S.C., Ybasco, et al. 1996) That means if we can develop hope within the context of human resources development, we can create a workforce of people who don't just have the willpower to succeed but also the waypower. They will have determination and "stick-to-it-ness," and the ability to see different solutions and find ways to remove obstacles to their goals.

Imagine the positive effects a "high-hope employee" could have on your workplace. They would find ways to achieve their goals and the best ways to achieve them too. Now imagine them with a high-hope leader. The effect would be even more powerful.

Signs of A High-Hope (high-H) Person

Anyone managing a team should be able to spot the high-H and low-H people on their team. High-Hs aren't the ones with a goofy smile on their face or an unrealistic attitude about life. They're evident by their realistic mindset and the way they approach problems. Some research even showed that high hopes have lower levels of anxiety. (Razlaff, 2017) They aren't necessarily the cheerleaders; they're the ones who see the forest through the trees and show everyone else the way out.

The people I've coached that I identify as high hopers can navigate intense situations better than others. They are unfazed by obstacles because their hopefulness leads them to think of another solution. When they find and implement that solution, they keep their expectations in check. They may acknowledge that things are not going well, but they are hopeful that with the right plan, things will be better on the other side.

Snyder noticed that high-H managers express "positive self-talk" such as "I can do this" or "I will not be stopped." (1) Hopeful people managers have a plan and can sell it to their team because of their hope. When the team members can see the manager's deep belief in the strategy they are presenting, they become inspired. The people manager motivates the team because they can paint a picture of what they can achieve with a new plan and perspective. They show their team a different path to their goal that has not been considered before.

This ability to be "planful" and have the "willpower" to find a solution is a key differentiator between the "hopeful" person and the "optimistic" one, according to Snyder. For example, let's examine the response of an optimistic manager versus a hopeful one during an economic downturn. The optimistic manager might delay labor lay-offs in favor of waiting to see what the economy will do. They have optimism that things are going to get better. On the other hand, a hopeful manager may pursue a new goal in response to the problem. For example, they may start identifying and pursuing creative ways of using the excess labor until the economy turns again. The hopeful manager shows the willpower to pursue an action and the ability to devise a plan. In other words, they demonstrate the waypower to achieve their goal.

Being hopeful also requires a bit of creativity to look at a problem differently to concoct a solution. I remember one hopeful manager I worked with (we'll call her Erica) who had an overflow of inventory, with aging stock in the storeroom as well. Sifting through the mounds of merchandise that had not been touched in years seemed like a hopeless task. Yet Erica tasked her supply chain leader to do it in a hopeful way. She turned a menial task into a treasure hunt and challenged them to find the oldest item in the storeroom. The team found a 15-year-old item and gave it a "retirement party" in celebration. Because of her hope that the project could be made somehow meaningful and fun, Erica took a hopeless-looking scenario and gave her team the willpower (motivation) to get the job done as well as the waypower (plan) to successfully complete it.

Hopefulness is also distinctly different, although related, to self-efficacy, the "E" in our HEROic model. Psychologist Albert Bandura explored this through a meta-analysis of 114 studies. (Luthans & Jensen, 2002) At first glance, the hopeful manager's attitude about finding an alternative solution seems similar to the self-efficacy of a manager who has confidence that their set plan will work. Both believe they are capable of the task at hand and will succeed. However, Bandura pointed out a difference between their expectations. "Efficacy expectations" are based on a person's confidence to perform a task, while "outcome expectations" of the hopeful person are based on the belief that a particular action will create a specific outcome. (Luthans & Jensen, 2002) In contrast, high-E and high-H people see the same blueprint, but the high-E has the confidence to build the house themselves. The high-H has the confidence to successfully manage a construction team to build the house.

Signs of a Low-Hope Manager

Nobody likes to see themselves as someone with low hope, yet I have met many people who could only be described that way. In the example above, if Erica had been a low-H manager, she would have looked at the task before her team as a mind-numbing waste of time. She would not have celebrated a 15-year-old item but instead regarded it as proof that the problem was even more significant than initially expected.

Low-H managers rarely see a way out of a situation. They resign themselves to a specific state of confusion or chaos, which ultimately keeps them from seeing the possibilities and making a plan to move forward.

Low-H managers are also often blamers. They see the problem as beyond them and beyond their control. In their view, the problem is the supply chain, the recession, or the drop in the workforce. In their opinion, there's nothing anyone can do. This is not to say that there may be existing factors beyond their control that impede success. There may be real obstacles that ultimately influence anyone's lack of success. However, for the low-H manager, searching for a solution stops there. They won't keep looking for solutions like the high-H manager will.

Low-H managers are typically resistant to change. Again, they typically find it difficult to embrace a new solution because they lack the vision to see how things improve. They will recognize and gravitate towards the reasons the solution won't work rather than how it possibly could. Their lack of hope affects their overall mindset.

Most people would rather work with a high-H rather than a low-H manager. The reality, though, is most of us must work with both at one time or another in our careers!

Hope Can Be Measured

So, is there a way to "measure" our amount of hope? Yes! Many researchers have successfully assessed an individual's level of hope, including Snyder. He developed an assessment known as the 12-item Adult Dispositional Hope Scale, which measured the self-reported hopefulness traits of an individual. Respondents rated their agreement on an eight-point scale from "definitely false" to "definitely true" regarding some statements, such as "I energetically pursue my goals." Although the score of participants fluctuated over time, it varied around the mean level of the individual's dispositional hope score, demonstrating that people have a measurable amount of hope.

Why Manager Hope is Important

Does a manager's level of hope affect their team? Many studies have shown the positive impact of hope in the workplace. For example, a study by Snyder of U.S. firms ranging from 8 to 40,000 employees showed that higher-H human resources produce more profit, have higher retention rates, and enjoy greater levels of employee satisfaction and commitment. (2)

However, the body of work by Chen (Chen, 2015) concentrated on leaders specifically and how their PsyCap affects their followers. He collected data in three phases from multiple sources, including 60 leaders and 319 followers from a telecom company in Taiwan. In this multi-level study, a team had to consist of a minimum of three people reporting to a common leader. Information was collected multiple times to avoid method variance problems. There were three-time intervals for data to be collected, spread 12 to 15 weeks apart.

Surveys were sent directly to participants. Leaders' average age was 48 years with approximately 22 years of experience. 70% of the leaders were male and 95% were college graduates. The followers averaged 40 years of age; 54% were female, and 76% were college graduates.

The results of the study proved all of Chen's hypotheses, which included (1) that a leader's PsyCap is a significant predictor of follower PsyCap (2) a leader's PsyCap is positively related to follower PsyCap; (3) Job engagement and follower PsyCap have a positive relationship, and (4) An individual's PsyCap is significantly related to their job engagement. Additionally, job engagement showed a significant relationship with task performance. The findings furthered the understanding of how leader PsyCap can impact follower performance. Therefore, we can reasonably conclude that PsyCap should be a required capability of a leader. (Chen, 2015)

Studies have also shown that training interventions in "hope" for employees can be very effective and create a more focused, hope-filled workforce. (Luthans & Jensen, 2002) We have learned that hope is something anyone can develop. Therefore, the high-H manager who can share their experience can provide interventions for their team to raise performance along with everyone's level of hope.

High-H managers will be motivated to try to influence the level of hope in their team members. However, even managers who need to boost their own hope levels can benefit from using some of the techniques offered by Luthans and Jensen to boost hope levels in their teams. The researchers offer these suggestions based on their research and experience:

Specific goal setting. This means setting goals that are challenging and include numbers, percentages, and target dates to help clarify goals across the team.

Breaking down goals. Snyder called it the "stepping method," and it is a way to guide your team through more actionable, attainable goals.

Developing contingency pathways. Hopeful people see more than one way to achieve a goal. Defining these alternatives in advance, with an accompanying action plan, will help the team stay hopeful.

Acknowledge the positive in the process. Celebrate the small goals that the team achieves along the way to the big ones. Doing so keeps the team from focusing on the final goal and keeps them motivated for the next milestone.

Be prepared to persist. Set realistic expectations. There may be problems along the way, but they can be overcome with persistence.

Practice "what ifs." After developing your contingency plans, know in advance which ones you would best implement in the face of different obstacles. Talk through scenarios and "what ifs" to know which path to take if the need arises.

Know when to "Re-goal." Team leaders should not encourage "false hope" in their team. When alternative paths and persistence have failed or will imminently fail, it is time to reconsider and retool the goals in place.

Interventions like these can help increase the personal hopefulness of the individual team members and increase the manager's level of hopelessness too!

How High is Your Hope?

By now, you may be wondering how you fare on the hope scale. You may even wonder if you are indeed as hopeful as you think you are if given a "hope" assessment. Knowledge is always power when it comes to our PsyCap!

Knowing that you are a hopeful person does not mean you will never have moments of hopelessness. Although we all have a baseline of hope, there will always be times in our life when we will feel more "hopeless" than others.

For me, it was when my mother died. I have always been a high-H, positive person, so others noticed a marked difference in my behavior when I plummeted to a dark, hopeless place to mourn her passing properly. I was working on my dissertation at the time, which was a work she inspired but would never see. I gave myself permission to rest, but then knew I had to rise. It was not easy to return to my research. Staying depressed would have been easier. Depression is the easiest place to live because it is comfortable in the moment of sorrow. The hard part is pushing against the comfortable to attain a more uncomfortable, but ultimately superior result. However, this is precisely what a hopeful person does when they hit a difficult situation. They recognize that giving up is the easy choice. They persevere. So, I did as well and finished my dissertation on the topic you are currently reading about.

Today there are multiple PsyCap measurements to measure hope, as well as the other PsyCap competencies. The original questionnaire was a PCQ-24 published by Mind Garden (Luthans et al 2014), consisting of a 24-question self-reporting measure that includes six items to measure each of the four resources (Luthans & Youssef-Morgan, 2017). Researchers developed it to reveal the return on investment for PsyCap interventions and make it an attractive tool to be used by human resource departments (Luthans F., 2007) In my own study of all four of the HERO competencies, I used an abbreviated version called the PCQ-12

Later, another study on PsyCap led to the development of an assessment to measure implicit psychological constructs (Harms, 2012) and introduced the I-PCQ, or Implicit Psychological Capital Questionnaire. The I-PCQ differs from the original PCQ because it is not solely a self-report instrument. It asks that other acquaintances of the participant rate the participant's PsyCap. I-PCQ hoped to eliminate common method variance in the standard PCQ (Newman, 2014) but was unsuccessful.

For our purpose, I have developed an even smaller, five-question, self-assessment for each of the competencies. The assessment questions get to the heart of whether you are a "low" or "high" hope leader. Be honest with yourself. Remember that even should you discover that you are a low-H individual or team leader, there is plenty you can do to develop it further. Everyone can work towards being the perfect HEROic leader, one letter at a time!

HEROic ASSESSMENT:
Part 1: HOPE

Below is a brief assessment based on the advanced ones used by Chen and Luthans in their studies. As you progress through this book and learn about the different constructs of HERO in detail, you will see similar assessments at the end of each of the chapters that cover competencies. Answer the questions in each assessment and keep a running tally of where you fall on each scale in the table provided in Appendix 2. You can then add up your score and find out where you are on the HEROic scale and how to concentrate your efforts to lift your leadership based on the constructs of PsyCap.

Read each question and rate your answer 1 – 6 to correspond with your answer:

Strongly Disagree	Disagree	Somewhat Disagree	Agree	Strongly Agree
1	2	3	4	5

1. I feel I am basically successful as a leader of my team.

   1   2   3   4   5

2. I have set goals with my team and am motivated to pursue them.

   1   2   3   4   5

3. My team meets the goals that are set for them.

   1   2   3   4   5

4. As a leader, I believe there are many ways to solve any problem.

   1   2   3   4   5

5. My team and I have more than one solution to every problem.

   1   2   3   4   5

COMPETENCY	SUM OF POINTS FROM ASSESSMENT
Hope	

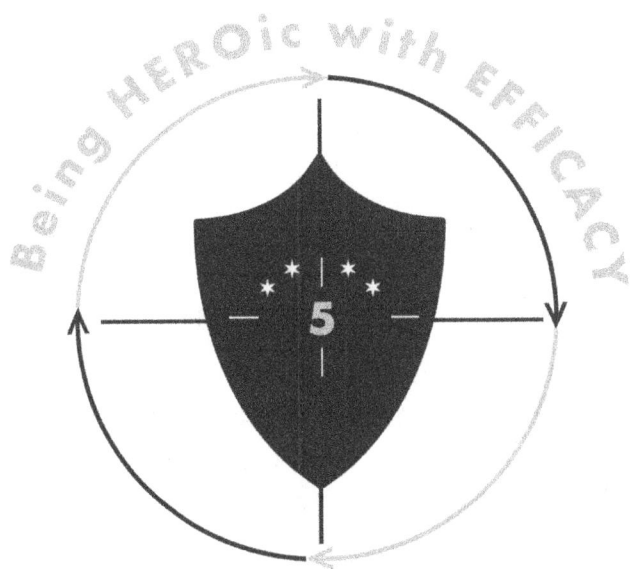

Being HEROic with EFFICACY

5

Chapter 5

Being HEROic with SELF-EFFICACY

The "E" in HERO stands for self-efficacy. Self-efficacy isn't a word you use every day, but self-efficacy is necessary for team leaders and their team members to perform at their best.

As part of HERO, the resource of self-efficacy centers around a person's belief in their ability to complete a task or meet a goal. The noted psychologist, Albert Bandura, first defined self-efficacy as a resource of PsyCap. (Sable et al., 2008). His work on self-efficacy began in 1977 and spanned over 20 years. Bandura's concept of self-efficacy refers to specific situations in which individuals must make judgments about their ability to complete a task. (Sable et al., 2008). For example, an employee with high self-efficacy (a high-E) who is presented with a problem with several solutions will be able to determine the best one for the job. Then they'll go on to complete the task. Bandura also found that self-efficacious employees are likely to be more engaged at work. That's because having the resource of self-efficacy leads to a willingness to spend energy on tasks and complete them. (Schaufeli and Salanova, 2007)

Larson & Luthans defined self-efficacy as the measure of someone's ability to take on a task and their willingness to put in the necessary work to complete the task (Larson & Luthans, 2007). So not only will a high-E team member take responsibility for an assignment, but they have the drive to complete it. Also, like the other resources in the HERO model (hope, resilience, and optimism), self-efficacy is a state-like construct that is open to development (Luthans, Avolio, Avey, & Norman, 2007). This is good news for high-E leaders who want to see more self-efficacy from their team members!

Self-Efficacy and Positive Psychology

Self-efficacy is rooted in positive psychology and the power of positive emotions. Psychologist Barbara Fredrickson took a closer look at this relationship and developed the "broaden-and-build" theory of positive emotions. Her approach, which has been supported through extensive research, looks at discrete positive emotions—including interest, contentment, and pride. Her theory states that having positive emotions will broaden people's thought-action repertoires or the feelings that widen the subject's possible thoughts and actions. For example, the positive emotion of interest broadens the urge to explore and take in new information and experience. The positive feeling of contentment creates the urge to savor current life circumstances and integrate them into new views of self and the world. Likewise, the positive emotion of pride, spawned from successful personal achievements, helps us envision even more extraordinary achievements in the future. (Fredrickson, 2001) She concludes that positive emotions are worth cultivating to flourish and build enduring physical, intellectual, social, and psychological resources. All of these resources are related to the development of our self-efficacy.

Bandura broke out self-efficacy into three specific dimensions based on cognitive social theory: (a) the difficulty of the task (level or magnitude), (b) the strength of certainty someone has (to perform a particular level of task difficulty), and (c) generality (the extent to which magnitude and strength beliefs generalize across tasks and situations). (Bandura, 1986, 1997). In general, self-efficacy is lower in people faced with completing a brand-new task rather than one they have done for years. However, people with a great deal of self-efficacy will more easily attempt challenging and uncomfortable tasks, especially if they have tried something similar before.

Bandura's focus on self-efficacy took "situational demands" into account and gave it a more narrow focus as a task-specific or state-like construct known as Specific Self-Efficacy (SSE). (Chen, Gully, & Eden, 2001) Many researchers have measured SSE through assessments, but it was the team of Chen, Gully & Eden who put forth a more general measuring tool for general self-efficacy (GSE). They concluded a marked difference between SSE and GSE. (Chen, Gully, & Eden, 2001) SSE is believed to concern our motivational state, or ability to complete a specific task. At the same time, GSE is a motivational trait pertaining to our belief in our "overall competence to effect requisite performances across a wide variety of achievement situations." (Judge, Erez, et al., 1998, p. 170).

Several researchers have determined that the most powerful antecedent of GSE is the aggregation of previous experiences. (Chen, Gully, & Eden, 2001) In other words, our self-efficacy increases as we live and acquire more experiences. However, Bandura asserted that achieving something we never thought possible can be a transformative experience and change our overall beliefs in our efficacy. (Chen, Gully, & Eden, 2001)

GSE: Origin and Growth

Our GSE is a fundamental part of us that can be developed in childhood. A look at GSE in students shows us that self-efficacy is one of the foundational resources youngsters need to succeed. In his Student Motivation and Engagement Wheel, Andrew Martin spoke of several factors that underpin student engagement. These included *booster cognitions*, which help students adapt; *booster behaviors* which help students succeed; *mufflers*, which impede learning; and *maladaptive dimensions* ("guzzlers"), which handicap and disengage students. He lists self-efficacy as one of the booster cognitions, alongside value of work and mastery orientation. (Martin, 2005)

According to Martin, one way to increase self-efficacy is through personal bests (PBs). When we achieve a personal best, we prove to ourselves that success is accessible. Therefore, the more we pursue PBs and have the opportunities to do so, the more we can enhance our self-efficacy. (Martin, 2005)

In my managerial consulting work, I've found that team members most appreciate people managers who push them to be their best--leaders who challenge and stretch their teammates to do more than they have ever done before. When teammates succeed, they experience positive feelings of excitement, accomplishment, and fearlessness to conquer the next big challenge.

To encourage your team to achieve more PBs, Martin offers a four-factor model of assigning goals that are specific, challenging, competitively self-referenced, and based on self-improvement. He suggests fostering a commitment to PBs at an organizational level and helping employees set and attain PBs within the context of their work. Managers who encourage their team to achieve more PBs will grow self-efficacy in the team members, which will ultimately translate to better on-the-job performance.

High-E and Plasticity

Have you ever noticed how some people are easily influenced while others aren't? Researchers have looked at self-efficacy and the "behavioral plasticity" theory. The word "plasticity" refers to how easily influenced a person is by outside events. Research has shown that people with low self-esteem are more likely to have plasticity. They are more likely to be influenced by external factors and more malleable in their attitudes. In social situations, this can be detrimental. In the workplace, it can be beneficial when it comes to interventions (Saks & Ashforth, 2000).

For example, people assessed with low GSE are typically influenced by workplace interventions and training more than those with high GSE. One job search training intervention improved the re-employment of low GSE participants but not those with high GSE. Researchers Eden and Zuk did a study involving an intervention to reduce seasickness in naval cadets. The low GSE cadets were influenced more by the intervention than the high GSE cadets were. In both these studies, the low GSE participants had more room for improvement from the intervention. (Saks & Ashforth, 2000)

Meanwhile, individuals with a high degree of GSE (and probable accompanying high self-esteem) may not be as affected by interventions but are most likely more protected from adverse and potentially ego-shattering events. (Chen, Gully, & Eden, 2001) They will also be more highly engaged at work and have more task involvement and absorption. (Schaufeli and Salanova, 2007)

Measuring GSE

The first type of assessment introduced for the SSE was the Sherer et al. 17-item General Self-Efficacy Scale (SGSE). The assessment measures "a general set of expectations that the individual carries into a new situation." (Sherer et al. 1982). More recently, a new general self-efficacy scale known as the NGSE was validated by research from a team of psychologists across two countries. (Chen, Gully, & Eden, 2001).

The idea to develop a new scale was fueled by criticism from other researchers, including Bandura. Some researchers questioned the distinction between self-esteem and GSE and the ability of GSE to predict behavior. (Chen, Gully, & Eden, 2001) It was easier to recognize and measure behavioral outcomes with SSE assessments since the research included specific tasks, for example, i.e., how to operate the specific computer software. (e.g., Martocchio & Judge, 1997) Because of this, GSE should not be regarded as a substitute or replacement for SSE but rather a supplement to help predict performance. (Chen, Gully, & Eden, 2001) Also, with the complexity of today's organizations, employees with high GSE can sustain their motivation and buffer themselves from failure during stressful times in the workplace.

The new NGSE developed an 11-item instrument with seven items diverging from the Rosenberg Self-Esteem Scale and SGSE scale. It addressed the criticism that self-efficacy and self-esteem were regarded and measured similarly. The new scale also predicted SSE and moderated the influence of previous performance on subsequent SSE, whereas self-esteem and the SGSE scale did not. (Chen, Gully, & Eden, 2001). The team performed three studies to verify the new scale of measurement. The raw data and statistical modeling of the results proved that the predictive validity of the NGSE scale was higher than that of the SGSE. Another study used a Hebrew version of the scale on an Israeli population. The results replicated findings that the predictive validity of the NGSE scale, even in Hebrew, was somewhat higher than the Hebrew SGSE scale, which showed the NGSE to be a shorter and more valid measure of the GSE than the SGSE. (Chen, Gully, & Eden, 2001)

Using the correct assessment and measurement, team leaders can empower themselves with predictive information about how their employees will react to interventions in the workplace. (Martin, 2005)

Signs of a High-E Manager

Not only can you spot a person with high general self-efficacy by how they approach problems, set goals, and achieve, but also by how they evaluate themselves. Researchers have found that our GSE affects our worldview in many ways (Shelton, 1990; Sherer et al., 1982). These include:

Our self-esteem. The more we can achieve and experience success rather than failure, the less harshly we will judge ourselves. A high-E person accepts their mistakes and is confident they will do better next time.

Locus of control. We can alter our feelings about how much control we have over our lives by setting a goal and reaching it. Even in seemingly hopeless situations, high-E people try to find some control over any situation. They believe they make their destiny; they do not feel they are at the mercy of fate.

[71]

Neuroticism. GSE opposes the impact of negative emotions like anger, anxiety, self-consciousness, irritability, emotional instability, and depression on our lives. It allows us to accept and sustain positive emotions in tumultuous times. To the outside world, high-E people may appear positive and happier than other people.

Goal orientation.

People with high GSE tend to be more goal-oriented and more successful in reaching those goals. They understand setting goals is the first step to achievement, so goal setting comes naturally to them.

High-E managers also understand the importance of celebration. Taking time to acknowledge and commemorate the team's achievements creates positive feelings that are so important to self-efficacy. Celebration elevates the team, especially if the celebration is approved and known to upper management.

Signs of a Low-E Manager

I once worked with a manager (who we'll call Marie) who was a "low-E" and struggled with her self-efficacy. She joined the company as a start-up, and worked her way into her current position, improving processes along the way and becoming instrumental in the company's rapid growth. By all measures, Marie had achieved and exceeded many of her PBs along the way, but she would not acknowledge it. She would minimize her contribution and attribute the company's growth to other factors besides her efforts. "We just grew organically," she would say. Over the years, Marie was asked to address upper management and share her knowledge and abilities, yet she always avoided the opportunity. She regularly flees the spotlight.

The challenge with Low-E managers like Marie is that the team suffers because of them. If the manager cannot elevate themselves, they will be less likely to elevate their team. For Marie's employees who are working hard and not being acknowledged by upper management, the lack of appreciation became frustrating. Marie was not reporting "up" and her team was being ignored by upper management. I told Marie she would not be in the position she was if she did not have the skills to get there. She needed to work on "communicating up" to make her superiors aware of her achievements and the work of her team too. It is especially important to do this in large organizations where work is often done in silos. If the manager doesn't elevate the team, the team's contribution to the company's broader mission will go unnoticed. Teammates will become disengaged, and in the worst cases, they may move on to another organization.

Advocating for yourself is very important for you and your team. It's the responsibility of a good manager and a natural activity for high-E managers. If you are a low-E manager, you may need to work on advocating for yourself and your team.

Signs of a (Too) High-E Manager

High-E is a valuable resource for any manager, but there is such a thing as a manager with "too much" self-efficacy. Letting superiors know about your team's achievements is a good thing, but managers must temper confidence with humility. Nobody likes a braggart or an obnoxious, self-serving leader. Nobody likes a leader who elevates themselves and nobody else. And you never want your teammates to resent you or hope your idea fails in order to teach you a lesson.

High confidence and high competence are never a ticket to infallibility. The high-E and (too) high-E manager will fail but will do so with resilience and optimism. Typically, they will report the failure to the boss with a revised plan and an amended goal to yield the same result. They are optimistic that they will resolve an issue, whatever it is.

Whether soaring like an eagle or picking up the pieces of a failure, the high-E manager can be a pleasure to work for as long as they include their team in the accolades. That's why it's essential for high-E managers to be vigilant and be sure to elevate their team members as vigorously as they elevate themselves.

High-E managers have the ability to build a high-E team. Are you a high-E manager? Find out.

HEROic ASSESSMENT:
Part 2: SELF-EFFICACY

Below is a brief assessment based on the advanced ones used by Chen and Luthans in their studies. As you progress through this book and learn about the different constructs of HERO in detail, you will see similar assessments at the end of each of the chapters that cover competencies. Answer the questions in each assessment and keep a running tally of where you fall on each scale in the table provided in Appendix 2. You can then add up your score and find out where you are on the HEROic scale and how to concentrate your efforts to lift your leadership based on the constructs of PsyCap.

Read each question and rate your answer 1 – 5 to correspond with your answer:

Strongly Disagree	Disagree	Somewhat Disagree	Agree	Strongly Agree
1	2	3	4	5

1. I feel confident assessing business problems and proposing solutions.

1	2	3	4	5

2. I feel confident in presenting my work area to senior leaders.

1	2	3	4	5

3. I feel confident sharing my thoughts on strategic initiatives.

1   2   3   4   5

4. I feel confident setting goals and objectives in my work area.

1   2   3   4   5

5. I feel confident connecting with internal and external stakeholders for advice when I have a problem..

1   2   3   4   5

COMPETENCY	SUM OF POINTS FROM ASSESSMENT
Efficacy	

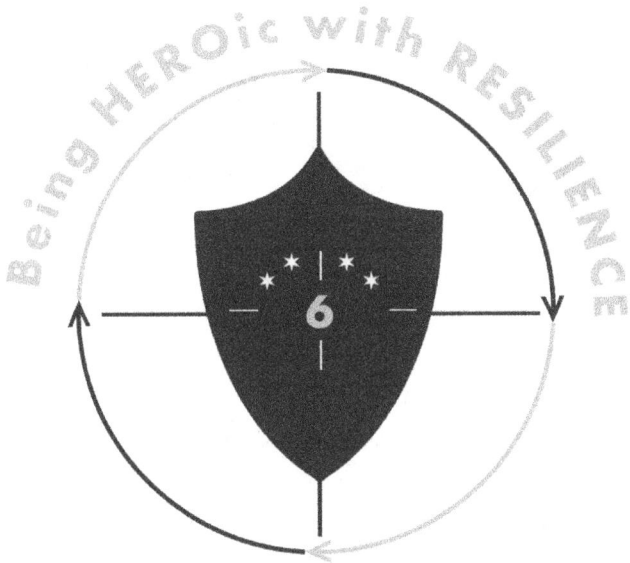

Being HEROic with RESILIENCE

6

Chapter 6

Being HEROic with RESILIENCE

When I hear the word "resilience," I think of a rubber band. When you were a child, you undoubtedly tested a rubber band, stretching it as far as it would go just to see what would happen. You would stretch it almost to its breaking point. Then, with wonder, you'd let it go and watch it snap back to its original shape. It looked exactly the same as it did before you overstretched it. It was invincible. In fact, that rubber band looked all ready to be overstretched once again.

Don't we wish we were all like that? Resilient like a rubber band? I imagine you understand what I'm saying. Everyone has experienced a stressful situation that has made us feel uncomfortable and has stretched us until we felt like we were reaching our breaking point. It could be family stress like I experienced when my mother was sick and fading away. Or it can be stress at work, like a ruthless boss, an anticipated firing or layoff, a hostile corporate takeover, or facing the closing of a business. Any of these can stretch us to our emotional limits. Chances are that whatever we endured in the past, whether or not it was in our control, once the pressure was finally released and we snapped back into place, we were not the same, like a rubber band. The experience probably changed us in some way, either positively or negatively.

Resilience is the degree to which we bounce back and continue to function after a stressful episode. Resilience is not only a sought-after skill; it is the third essential PsyCap resource, the "R" in HERO, and an absolute must for the HEROic leader.

What is Resilience?

The positive psychologist Fred Luthans defined resilience as "the developable capacity to rebound or bounce back from adversity, conflict, failure or even positive events, progress, and increased responsibility." (Luthans & Jensen, 2002) Resilience was once thought to be a personality trait that was rare and elusive. However, research on resilience in schizophrenic mothers and their children found that children could be resilient, regardless of their conditions. (Luthar, Cicchetti, & Becker, 2000) However, a later study found that three factors may affect the development of resilience: (1) attributes of the children themselves; (2) aspects of their families, and (3) characteristics of their wider social environments. (Masten & Garmezy, 1985; Garmezy, 1971).

Researchers concluded that resilience is not a rare personality trait. Instead, like the other resources of PsyCap, it has been empirically proven to be state-like and able to be developed. (Luthans, 2007).

In the workplace, resilience is not merely reactive; it can be proactive and grow as an individual goes through various situations in life (Youssef & Luthans, 2007a). Hope, optimism, and resilience all share these characteristics. With our own motivation, each PsyCap resource can have an impact on job performance and attitudes at work (Youssef & Luthans, 2007a). That means we can work on our resilience and create a better environment for ourselves on the job.

The Traits of Resilience

Are we born resilient? Or do we have resilience thrust upon us? Researchers have looked at this question from all angles.

One research report dived into character strengths and how they predict a person's resilience. (Martinez-Marti, 2016) The researchers observed six distinct factors related to resilience-- positive affect, self-efficacy, optimism, social support, self-esteem, and life satisfaction—that had a more significant relationship with resilience than risk factors. They hypothesized that further development of resilience might be more effective than reducing the risk factors. (Martinez-Marti, 2016) To begin their research, they looked at the VIA (Values in Action) inventory proposed by Peterson and Seligman (2004). The VIA classified six virtues (wisdom, knowledge, courage, humanity, justice, temperance, and transcendence) and 24 distinct character strengths under each one. The character strengths included traits such as curiosity, bravery, zest (for life), self-regulation, hope, religiousness, interpersonal, etc. They hypothesized that all the traits would somehow correlate to resilience, and the results of their study of 363 people proved their hypothesis. All the strength factors yielded significant positive correlations with the six resilience-related factors, except the strength of interpersonal and theological, which only correlated significantly with a few of the strengths. (Martinez-Marti, 2016)

The three strengths that showed the most significant correlation with resilience were hope, zest, and bravery, with bravery leading the pack. This correlates with research from several other psychologists, including Hutchinson, Stuart, & Pretorius (2010) and Jordan (2005,) who believe that resilience involves the development of courage, especially related to the recovery of life satisfaction after physical illness.

On the job, a resilient leader must often be brave to do what is necessary for the good of the organization. I'm reminded of a leader I coached, who I'll call Rosie. She was a successful manager who had her budget slashed by upper management. Rosie was forced to make staff cuts, which was very painful and difficult to do. She had always worked at financially healthy organizations, and overseeing layoffs was a new experience. However, Rosie was a resilient leader, so instead of wasting time questioning the decision, she immediately began replanning sessions to determine a strategy. In the end, she did what the organization wanted and didn't shrink from facing her staff. Rosie put energy into keeping them hopeful and motivated to retain them, knowing more work would now be required from a smaller staff.

The researchers looking at character strengths concluded that different strengths promote resilience differently. (Martinez-Marti, 2016) Emotional strengths give individuals energy, determination, and social connectedness to face adversity. For example, a trusted friend who reminds you of your self-worth on the job can help you become resilient in a challenging workplace situation. Strengths of restraint might help individuals become more resilient by helping them accomplish goals in difficult situations and regulate emotions in ways that promote positive adaptation and good decision-making, such as learning to live on a budget after losing a job. Intellectual strengths may involve the use of information in new ways for better problem-solving. For example, someone might launch a new business after being let go from a job. And finally, interpersonal strengths promote resilience by keeping relationships healthy and facilitating the organization and occurrence of group activities, regardless of the challenges. An example would be Rosie, who pulled together and motivated her team in a difficult situation. (Martinez-Marti, 2016)

Resilience and Positive Psychology

Resilience has a definite relationship with positive psychology and organizational behavior in the workplace, and there has been a plethora of research on the relationship between employee behaviors and outcomes. (Sun Yung & Hyun Yoon,

2015). One study consisted of a voluntary survey administered to hotel employees in Seoul. The survey was translated from English to Korean. (A pilot test ensured the scale's reliability). The survey used a seven-point Likert scale to report a degree of agreement with statements adapted from previous researchers. The study found that the PsyCap of the employee had a significant, positive effect on job satisfaction, organizational citizenship behaviors, and resiliency. In fact, resilience helped participants overcome frustration and provided increased opportunities for growth (Sun Yung & Hyun Yoon, 2015). Such growth can often include the resource of resiliency itself.

A recent research report published in the UK (Baker & Baker, 2021) introduced a skills-based model of personal resilience inspired by positive psychology for training people in resilience. The model touches upon three domains: cognitive, behavioral, and emotional. The researchers believe the model contributes to growth at different stages of the resilience cycle, which include initial survival of adversity, recovery, resuming normal function and emotional stability, and psychological development and thriving. Resilience is associated with successfully regulating stress and obtaining a good balance of "positive" and "negative" emotions. "Cognitive flexibility," or the ability to adjust our thinking from old situations to new ones, can also help us become more resilient. (Moore & Malinowski, 2009) Resilient people tend to be good at forming social connections and using them to manage new challenges and their emotional reactions to them. (Ozbay, et al., 2007) In this way, a person's ability to create and nurture relationships can help them develop their overall resiliency.

Developing Resilience

The skills-based model of resilience (Baker & Baker, 2021) also addresses the sympathetic nervous system, the fight or flight response, and how resilient people react in a crisis. The model teaches people the importance of recognizing and managing threat responses and calming their sympathetic nervous system arousal. It also encourages the building of positive emotions and explores ways to develop and understand good social connections and emphasizes the importance of trust in developing relationships. Reciprocal giving and receiving of support is also part of the model. The researchers believe that if individuals develop these skills, they can influence functioning at different stages of the stress response. They will be able to build resilience capacity at the moment that can eventually lead to survival, recovery, and thriving. (Baker & Baker, 2021) Other resilient behaviors that teach people to recover from episodes of stress include taking time out, switching tasks, engaging in relaxation and mindfulness, exercising, and maintaining participation in hobbies and special interests. (Baker & Baker, 2021)

Resilience has a lot to do with mindset, and your mindset can help build your resilience. We can choose how we bounce back and adapt to adversity. It's not about the adversity---whether big or small—it's the way we manage it that counts. For example, I worked with someone at a high level who we'll call Anne. Anne told me that her manager had continually passed her up for promotions at her previous job, and said that she would never manage at a higher level. The advice stuck in her head and shook her confidence. But because she was resilient, Anne was able to reverse the situation. She investigated why she had been passed over and worked to overcome her professional shortcomings. She stayed with the organization for a few more years, and when the time was right, she moved to another organization at a level that her manager predicted she would never reach. Anne's mindset was to achieve her goal, which fueled her resilience.

Our previous experiences, whether good or bad, undeniably affect our resilience. We learn resiliency through competition and the advantages and disadvantages we are handed in life. I've administered behavioral assessments for PsyCap that involved hours of interviews with participants, following a questionnaire asking about their earliest influences and mentors to find out how those relationships affected their PsyCap. Our experiences make a difference. However, whether our experiences make us more resilient or timid, we can always build on our personal resources.

Signs of a High-R Leader

Many leaders don't show their resiliency until adversity hits. When it does, you can tell a high-R leader by the way they handle problems. High-R Leaders are doers. If you knock them down, they don't spend time on the floor. They hop back up and begin planning their way out of any unpleasant situation.

High-R leaders may be highly successful or moderately competent. Success isn't a requisite for a resilient manager but being resilient gives them an advantage in the workplace. As in the example of Anne, leaders with resilient mindsets can find opportunities to turn around misfortune through problem-solving or determination. If they also have bravery, their courage bolsters their resiliency and encourages them to follow a new, audacious plan that may make a difference for the organization.

The Low-R Leader

I once met a leader who we'll call Joel. Joel claimed that all his experiences at work had been positive ones. He claimed that he had never had a bad experience at work. Looking at him, you could see why. He was highly successful, a superstar on his team, and he never failed to deliver. In Joel's case, he didn't know if he was resilient; his resiliency had never been tested.

As a coach, I warned Joel to prepare for the day he would experience failure and have to call upon his resilience. It's not that I wished him harm or felt his career was on a downslide, but few people get through their careers without at least one negative experience. I wanted him to be prepared. I tried to get him to agree to work on his resiliency proactively, before he needed it. I was then confident that when adversity struck, Joel would be ready and have the resilience to lead his team through any fire.

The interesting truth is that a low-R leader is unpredictable. As they have never called their resiliency into service, it is hard to predict how the low-R leader will manage when a crisis hits their team. The low-R leader y may have a track record of being resilient elsewhere, but if not, the team will not know what to expect should a challenge hit the organization. I hope Joel will be ready to tap into his resiliency reserves if and when it's necessary to lead his team through adverse circumstances. If you are a low-R leader, I wish the same for you too!

Whether we have been tested by fire and have the resilience of a rubber band or we've never lived an easy life without stress or worry, we all have some resilience. How and when we use it depends on our circumstances. Yet it's essential for every leader to become resilient for their good and the good of the teams they lead.

HEROic ASSESSMENT:
Part 3: RESILIENCE

Below is a brief assessment based on the advanced ones used by Chen and Luthans in their studies. As you progress through this book and learn about the different constructs of HERO in detail, you will see similar assessments at the end of each of the chapters. Answer the questions in each assessment and keep a running tally of where you fall on each scale in the table provided in Appendix 1. You can then add up your score and find out where you are on the HEROic scale and how to concentrate your efforts to lift your leadership based on the constructs of PsyCap.

Read each question and rate your answer 1 – 5 to correspond with your answer:

Strongly Disagree	Disagree	Somewhat Disagree	Agree	Strongly Agree
1	2	3	4	5

1. I have trouble moving on after a setback at work.

1	2	3	4	5

2. I'm able to manage difficulties at work.

1	2	3	4	5

3. I can work independently, no matter what happens.

1	2	3	4	5

4. I don't let work stress get to me.

1	2	3	4	5

5. I've experienced difficulties at work before and can therefore get through them.

1	2	3	4	5

COMPETENCY	SUM OF POINTS FROM ASSESSMENT
Resilience	

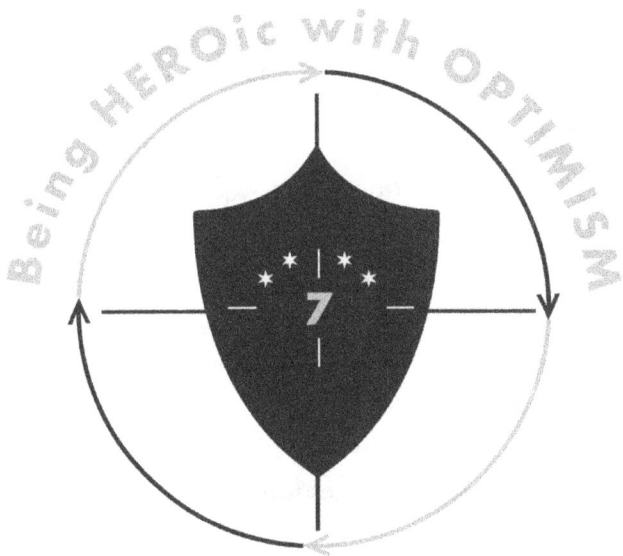

Being HEROic with OPTIMISM

7

Chapter 7

Being HEROic with OPTIMISM

When you hear the word "optimistic," what do you think about? Do you imagine someone with rose-colored glasses who always thinks everything is perfect? Or the person who perpetually sees the proverbial glass of water half full instead of half empty? While these examples might describe a type of optimism, the important part of optimism is having the right amount in our lives. When we do, optimism can be an extremely potent PsyCap resource.

Fred Luthans defined optimism as "a positive explanatory style that attributes positive events to personal, permanent, and pervasive causes and interprets negative events in terms of external, temporary, and situation-specific factors." (Youssef, 2007b) In other words, an optimistic person sees the world as inherently positive. They see adverse events as more of an occasional, situation-specific occurrence.

Put another way, optimistic individuals expect success (Avey, Hughes, & Norman, 2008). An optimistic person believes there will be a positive outcome even in the most stressful, unpleasant situations. A highly optimistic (or High-O) person takes personal responsibility for the positive outcomes in their lives (Avey, Hughes, & Norman, 2008) and demonstrates a belief that they can create their success (Avey, Luthans, & Mhatre, 2011). An optimistic person expects to be successful.

Like hope and resilience, optimism is an intentional, positive appraisal of situations based on self- motivation (Luthans, 2007).

Benefits of Optimism

Research has shown that optimism is not only good for your positive psychology but also for your health. People with high-O were found to have a quicker recovery from cardiac-related events, lower levels of distress (Brydon, Walker, Wawrzyniak, Chart, & Steptoe, 2009), improved survival rates for HIV (Ironson & Hayward, 2008), and a higher likelihood of engaging in healthy lifestyle choices (Schier & Carver, 1985) (Smith & MacKenzie, 2006) (Steptoe, Wright, Kunz-Ebrecht, & Iliffe, 2010) In general, optimists appear to be better at coping in times of distress too. (Andersson, 1996)

Pulling from positive psychology, Youssef and Luthans found a significant positive correlation between performance and PsyCap resources, including optimism. Optimism was among those resources which positively affect individuals behaviors and outcomes (Youssef, 2007b) and have a positive relationship with employee empowerment. It was one of the resources shown to be a stronger predictor for success than transformational leadership (Avey, Hughes, & Norman, 2008)

It is unsurprising that a high-O manager could have a positive effect on their team. I worked with a client we'll call George, who was definitely a high-O leader.

Among his team, his optimism was contagious. He felt the company could be successful, and others believed him. When the war in Ukraine hit and began to disrupt his manufacturing operation and supply chain, George met the challenge as a high-O manager would. Instead of panicking and laying off employees, he looked at how the current events would impact the plant in the long run. He devised a strategy to get through the next 12-24 months and put systems in place to find the right vendors and retailers to help him get his inventory out. Instead of having a knee-jerk reaction to the situation, George thought about how to mitigate its impact. He looked at his workforce and shuffled people to handle temporary roles to keep the operation moving forward. A manager like George, who's a high-O, can see beyond the short term, which can be a mighty powerful tool in business management.

Optimism works across many industries and work situations. A study of optimism in insurance agents found that optimistic agents were more successful. (Selig, 1986) Another study (Arakawa, 2007) found that positive project performance correlated significantly with the manager's optimism. In a study of Hungarian teachers to measure their PERMA, or five pillars of human flourishing (Positive emotions, Engagement, Positive Relationships, Meaning, and Accomplishment), optimism surfaced as one of the most relevant factors concerning workplace happiness. (Kun & Gadanecz, 2022) Referencing Fredrickson's broaden-and-build theory, the researchers acknowledged that their findings supported the idea that optimism can be increased with interventions and lead to more positive emotions, happiness, and well-being in their population of teachers.

Signs of a Low-O Manager

Just as the high-O manager positively impacts their team, the low-O manager can have a negative effect. The low-O manager sees the glass half empty, and their initial reaction to a problem is to see the worst-case scenario. I have worked with these leaders, too, and have seen how low-O can be detrimental to a team in two main ways:

Lack of communication. Low-O team members tend to be poor communicators. Because they feel there is nothing positive to report, they may fail to report altogether. Then when they leave their team in the dark, people tend to jump to negative conclusions. They create their own communication in the form of rumors and assumptions in the absence of communication from the top. If you're a low-O, stay alert to keep your communication up in as positive a manner as possible.

Operating from fear. Because Low-O managers may not be able to see the light at the end of a dark tunnel, they end up operating from a place of fear. This fear does not go unnoticed by the team. In many cases, it creates a domino effect of insecure feelings followed by assumptions. For example, a team member may leave because their role is unsuitable for them, but in response, the team creates rumors, based on fear that their teammate is leaving because the company is in trouble. It is the responsibility of the low-O manager to not only keep up communication with their team but also keep their team's fear under control as well.

Signs of a Too High-O Manager

If optimism is such a good thing and Low-O is dangerous, doesn't that mean the sky's the limit on "O" for team leaders? Not necessarily.

Team leads who operate from "too high-O" face challenges too. While starting from a place of high-O is almost always preferable than a place of low-O, leaders with too much optimism can fail to think realistically. It's okay and beneficial to believe that everything will be successful at the outset, but leaders must also be aware of both sides of every situation.

There are two main dangers of the manager with "too high-O":

Impaired decision-making. Some studies have shown that too much optimism can lead to poor decisions. For example, one study revealed that optimists are more likely than pessimists to continue betting even when they begin losing. (Gibson, 2004). Other research found that optimists are less likely to disengage when faced with an unattainable goal. (Andersson, 1996). Their ability to handle stress levels can be a personal asset but can also translate to an optimist not leaving a bad situation when they should.

Loss of credibility. I once worked with a "too High-O" financial services professional who we'll call Anne. She was a very successful closer and the architect of many multi-million-dollar deals. However, her team noticed that she seemed to focus on the potential positive outcomes of her proposals and tended to ignore the risks. With her optimistic mindset, she was prone to over-index the profitability of a deal. On many occasions, Anne failed to see the other side, and as a result, it affected her team's confidence in her. When she walked into the room, her team began to doubt that the deal she presented was the best. The team began to question her credibility. Anne needed to work on seeing the other side because she was *too* optimistic.

Handling Failure. Another danger of "too high-O" managers is that they are devastated and beside themselves when things don't turn out as planned. High-O leaders must temper their optimism with realism to prepare for the unexpected and not let it devastate them. For example, I'm writing this book and am optimistic it will be successful and sell a million copies, however if it doesn't, it won't destroy my self-esteem or send me into a deep depression. Someday, I'll write another book!

Although I mentioned evidence that optimism can have a positive impact on your health, optimism isn't necessarily healing. In fact some studies have shown that being too optimistic can compromise someone, particularly with health issues. Research has shown that over-optimism is associated with increased depression during post-cancer treatment for lung cancer survivors (Schofield, 2004). Increased optimism in cancer patients has also led to clinicians overestimating survival predictions.(Ingersoll et al., 2019) So it's clear that while optimism is a good thing, too much can be detrimental to reaching goals.

Raising Optimism

What can be done for the low-O manager? The only way to reverse the thinking of a low-O manager is to facilitate a true mindset shift. Low-O managers need to look at things through a different lens, which is very hard for them to do for several reasons.

First, telling a negative person not to be negative is problematic. The person needing to make the mind shift must believe and understand that the mindset shift is necessary for their increased well-being. Their initial reaction to the idea of working on their mindset will probably be, "That'll never work." (It's just their habit to say such things!) Change of any kind requires an open mind. If you can't get the low-O manager to make an effort to change, nothing will change.

For low-Os who want to change and are up for the challenge, they need to understand that it will take time and require a concerted effort and practice to break old habits. The process sounds simple, but for a low-O person, it is not. Let's try an example in which our low-O manager, Bill, has just been told the following:

"Bill, we're not going to make Q3 projections."

Bill is a Low-O so we know his first thoughts will be negative. Here are the steps Bill would have to take to create a mindset shift in this situation:

Step 1. Bill must acknowledge that the thought that just came into his head is negative. Before Bill can change, he must identify the problem. For most Low-Os, this means realizing that the negative thought comes naturally to them. In this example, Bill heard one statement and had the following thoughts: *We're going to have to begin lay-offs by the end of the year. I'm probably going to have to fire my best people. We'll have to call a meeting where I'll break the news.* As a negative thinker, these are the first and most likely thoughts to initially enter Bill's mind.

Step 2. Next, Bill must check the negative thought the minute it pops into his head. Typically, the negative thought of a low-O elicits feelings of fear, or anger, or hopelessness, just like this one did for Bill. To change, Bill must rebel against his thoughts! He needs to recognize that the "low-O" attitudes are kicking in and immediately eject them from his mind.

Step 3. Look at the thought through a different lens. In this step, Bill needs to think creatively to view the news more optimistically. It may be difficult for him, but instead of thinking about the potentially devastating effects of the information about Q3, Bill needs to reframe the information. For example, instead of thinking *that's terrible, what will we do?* Bill can think, *We can learn from this quarter. What should be our plan to regain earnings?*

But for the low-O manager, this is all easier said than done. Negative experiences shape low-O responses. The way to shift that perception is to focus on the differences between the past negative experiences and the present ones. For example, Bill might think, *Last time this happened, we didn't have the opportunities that we have today.* Situations are rarely identical, and the low-O manager is challenged with noticing what is different so they can proceed with confidence and optimism.

Optimism is an essential weapon in the HEROic leader's arsenal. Thankfully, like other resources of PsyCap, it is a resource that is not static and is able to be developed. Today's low-O can become tomorrow's high-O. I guarantee that leaders who become more optimistic will enjoy where that optimism will lead them!

HEROic ASSESSMENT:
Part 4 OPTIMISM

Below is a brief assessment based on the advanced ones used by Chen and Luthans in their studies. As you progress through this book and learn about the different constructs of HERO in detail, you will see similar assessments at the end of each of the chapters that cover competencies, like the one below. Answer the questions in each assessment and keep a running tally of where you fall on each scale in the table provided in Appendix 2. You can then add up your score and find out where you are on the HEROic scale and how to concentrate your efforts to lift your leadership based on the constructs of PsyCap.

Read each question and rate your answer 1 – 6 to correspond with your answer:

Strongly Disagree	Disagree	Somewhat Disagree	Agree	Strongly Agree
1	2	3	4	5

1. I expect the best to happen at work, even when I don't know what's around the corner.

1	2	3	4	5

2. If I'm in a position where something can go wrong, I think about it working out instead.

1	2	3	4	5

3. I'm optimistic about what will happen to me in the future at work.

1	2	3	4	5

4. Things usually happen the way I want them to in my job.

| 1 | 2 | 3 | 4 | 5 |

5. I can find the silver lining in almost every situation I encounter at work.

| 1 | 2 | 3 | 4 | 5 |

COMPETENCY	SUM OF POINTS FROM ASSESSMENT
Hope	
Efficacy	
Resilience	
Optimism	
SUM TOTAL	

YOU as a HEROic Manager

CHAPTER 8

YOU as a HEROic Manager

What manager wouldn't like to be known as HEROic?

In leadership development, labeling a manager as "heroic" is not new. However, "hero" behavior in leaders, as opposed to HEROic behavior, can be defined in many ways. Being a hero leader can be a help or a hindrance.

Author Chris Lowney wrote a successful book about Heroic Leadership in the Ignatian tradition. In his book, he explores four leadership themes, including heroism. His model of heroism is tied to self-motivation, stating that no mission is motivating until it is personal. Lowney believes heroism begins with each person considering, internalizing, and shaping their mission. (Lowney, Magis-Driven Heroic Leadership is a Daily Personal Pursuit, n.d.) Heroism means selflessly contributing to a greater goal. (Lowney, The Third Theme of Heroic Leadership: Heroism, 2011). In this context, heroism is selfless, not boastful. The hero serves others instead of being the one who takes all the glory.

The other end of the spectrum is the "hero" complex warned against by management consultants. The "hero complex" describes the leader who likes to save the day. They swoop in and bail their team out at the last minute on an ongoing basis. It's a type of hero behavior that ultimately builds a codependent team. The team knows the manager will always clean up their mess and fix anything that goes wrong. They become unmotivated to learn how to do things or improve processes because their leader is doing it all. However, codependence is rarely a good thing. Great leaders don't create a state of dependency in their teams; they empower them to do more independently. Rescuing is not leading. (Myatt, 2012)

The HEROic leader is vastly different from either of these heroes because their management style encompasses the four competencies of PsyCap. HEROic leadership stems from scientific research and its introduction into the corporate world. Mastering the competencies that HERO represents can help you become a better people manager. And if that is the goal, the first step is to learn more about yourself.

We congratulate you for doing this, because for many people, it's the most challenging part of becoming more HEROic! In an aircraft emergency you must don your own oxygen mask before you can help anyone around you. To develop a HEROic team, you must first understand your own strengths and weaknesses from the HEROic framework. Only then can you identify areas for improvement and strengths and seek development for even greater success in your organization.

At the end of chapters 3-7, we provided assessments to help you determine where you are on a scale of low to high for each of the HEROic competencies: Hope, Self-Efficacy, Resilience, and Optimism. Now, it is time to analyze your scores and see what wisdom you can find in what they reveal!

If you haven't done so, use the sheet in Book Appendix 2 to record your scores from your assessments at the end of each chapter. Add up your score for Hope, Efficacy, Resilience, and Optimism, and divide it by 4. This will give you your HERO score. use the key provided to determine whether you are low (L), medium (M), or high (H) for each HERO competency. The assessment is inspired by the PsyCap (PCQ 24) from Fred Luthans. The simple assessments in this book cannot take the place of the comprehensive surveys that were used in the studies often mentioned throughout this book. However, I used a nearly exact survey in my Ph.D. work that I described in the introduction.

From the chart in Appendix 2, you should be able to understand where you are "high" and "low." For convenience in reading this chapter, we've provided lines below to indicate your high (H), medium (M), or low (L) status for each of the competencies.

RESULTS OF MY HERO COMPETENCY ASSESSMENT

Complete the blank with an "H" for high, an "M" for medium, and "L" for low.

20-25 HIGH

12-19 MEDIUM

5 – 11 LOW

HOPE_____

EFFICACY _____

RESILIENCE ____

OPTIMISM _____

While it may seem that being "high" in everything means you're the perfect manager, that's not the case. In each of the competencies, being too high or too low can compromise your performance as a team leader. We all fall on a spectrum regarding character traits and competencies, and our position on the spectrum is fluid. At any time, we can work to improve our position with training and interventions, just as someone on a health spectrum can improve themselves with changes in exercise, diet, and quality health care. The goal is to reveal where you need to improve. Then, you can develop the competencies where you are "low "and make a more significant impact on your team.

High and Low Hope

If you scored high on the hope scale, congratulations. Having high hope is useful for a leader because it means that you can see the possibilities of the future, yet you are realistic about it. You have the planfulness and waypower to see tasks done with your team. While you may experience hopelessness in certain situations, you are better equipped than some people to see the positive that may lie ahead. Just monitor yourself to make sure that your hope is not TOO high. Overly high-H people can quickly lose sight of reality. Their hopefulness is too intense, and they can miss the necessity or opportunity to pivot business or activities to make the best decisions on behalf of their team.

On the other end of the spectrum, low-H managers can improve their levels of hope. They benefit from some consulting or intervention. There is usually a reason behind low-H and working with someone to understand and possibly reverse it is a wise decision. Managers with low-H can also benefit from employing some of the strategies presented in Chapter 4 to boost their hope. Specific goal setting, breaking down goals, developing contingency pathways, acknowledging the positive in the process, being prepared to persist, practicing "what ifs," and knowing when to "re-goal" are all concrete steps you can take to build your hope and become a better people manager in the process.

High and Low Self-Efficacy

If you are a high-E person, you exhibit a great deal of confidence in the workplace and probably in your personal life. Perhaps without knowing it, you are a product of the "broaden-and-build" theory of positive emotions discussed in Chapter 5, and your prior achievements help spur you on to tremendous success. You can not only strategize a way forward, but you can also take on the tasks yourself. You are no stranger to personal bests (PBs) and more than likely strive towards them at work and home. You see yourself in charge of what happens to you, and when you make a mistake, you keep moving, without letting failure steal your momentum. As a high-E manager, your biggest concern is to guard against your self-efficacy becoming "too" high. A manager whose "E" is "too high" will be seen as obnoxious, arrogant, or self-serving by their team. If you believe your "E" is off the charts, make sure you include your team in the accolades so that your success can boost them as well.

There are many reasons for low-E, including past experiences and management failure. However, ultimately the only person who can help grow your "E" is you. Managers can support and encourage you, but one tool you must develop is self-awareness. It is always helpful to reflect upon your achievements, as it is easy to forget what you achieved for your organization if you don't take stock now and then.

You must work to become aware of your accomplishments on the job and cultivate the habit of "communicating up." No matter what your role is in your company, you are contributing to a greater mission and should recognize your part in it.

High and Low Resilience

Resilience is one of those traits which is a true gift, and if you are a high-R, you undoubtedly have hope, zest, and bravery, as discussed in Chapter 6. You may be highly successful or moderately competent, but either way, your resilience in the face of obstacles keeps you and your team afloat when things get tough. Your bravery in the wake of challenging situations can inspire and motivate your team because instead of running away from problems, you run towards them with the self-confidence to be able to find a solution.

Is there a problem with being off-the-charts resilient? There can be. Some high-R leaders can procrastinate or "wing it" in certain situations because they are confident about recovering if something goes wrong. When high-R leaders lack a critical sense of urgency, they can unwittingly stress their team. This is especially true when the team members do not share the leader's level of resilience. When overly resilient leaders cannot build a parallel degree of resilience throughout their team, working with a high-R manager can be a constant, exhausting challenge for everyone involved. The team may feel like they are constantly putting out fires because their manager is not monitoring the deadlines and urgency of a project as they should.

Meanwhile, those on the lower end of the scale struggle with building up their resilience. As discussed in Chapter 6, the low-R manager can be unpredictable when adversity hits. The team will always wonder whether their team leader will face a challenge head-on or spend their time passing the buck. Because the leader is low-R, they could go either way. If you are a low-R who has never had to respond to adversity at work, it's important to develop your resilience *before* disaster strikes. You want to be a prepared leader for your team, with the strategies to weather whatever may come.

High and Low Optimism

High-O managers are a blessing to their teams. Their natural ability to see the sunny side of life can transform their team's attitude and spur it on to true success. As illustrated by the anecdote of George in Chapter 7, the high-O leader takes the negative in stride. Because their optimism allows them to see beyond the short-term, they make measured rather than impulsive decisions. Studies have shown that optimism is an important factor for on-the-job workplace happiness, so high-O leaders may appear happier in general than their co-workers. (Kun & Gadanecz, 2022)

However, there is absolutely a risk in being too "high-O." If you were looking for a "10" on the assessment and settled for marking yourself a "5," you may be a high-O leader with too much O. If that's the case, monitor yourself for those times when you may be letting your optimism blind you to reality. Like the high-stakes poker player who refuses to fold even though he's losing and only holding a pair of twos, you must control your natural inclination to keep going or stay the course when finding another path, or even giving up, might be the better decision. A leader who is overly optimistic can end up like Anne, whose anecdote in Chapter 7 illustrated how she lost credibility with her team for making too many improbable, impractical, overly-optimistic decisions.

If you score low on optimism, do not fear. Optimism can be increased with interventions and shifting your mindset. In most cases with low-O managers, the first line of defense is to capture and reframe the initial negative thoughts that arise with challenges. Low-Os must creatively transform the thoughts of "That'll never work" into "Will that work?" or, even better, "I think this will work!" It's easier than it sounds, but there are definite steps you can take to retrain your thoughts and achieve that critical mindset shift. It will ultimately help you view everything in a more optimistic way.

Adapting to Change

The great CEO Jack Welch said, "Change before you have to." It's a nod to how constant the need for change is in the workplace. To survive, we must be flexible to keep up with the times.

Everyone has some adaptability. How we adapt following a transformational event illustrates our resilience. How we adapt to change before an event occurs speaks to our flexibility, preparedness, and openness to change. The assessment you took from this book did not measure "openness to change" through a blunt question. However, let's suppose the assessment asked you to indicate your agreement with the statement, "I am open to change." What score would you give yourself? If your answer is lower than a "5," change itself may pose a challenge for you.

Even if you scored five points across the board, you would need to call upon all your HEROic resources to improve any of your HERO competencies because doing so requires an openness to change. Perhaps you identified that you possess "too much" of one competency and need to work on attaining balance with your other competencies. If you scored evenly across all the competencies, you might wonder where to start to become a more HEROic leader. Whether you need to supercharge a competency, dial it back, or sustain it, you must be open to changing yourself to become a better manager.

Through your exploration of the HERO competencies and your desire to improve yourself as a manager, I hope you find the openness to change what you must to become the best you can be. It may take a mindset shift, the summoning of bravery, or a good dose of humility to accept that change is necessary. Whatever it takes, any change you make to increase or stabilize your HEROic leadership competencies will be worth any sacrifice.

Value of a Truth Partner

You now have one piece of the puzzle that you need to become a more HEROic leader—you know where you stand on each of the competencies. From here, you have guidance throughout this book for building up your deficient competencies to become a better leader.

Another critical question is, "How will I know if I'm making progress?" That's where a truth partner comes in.

A truth partner is someone familiar with your leadership who would be willing to help keep you accountable regarding your work in becoming a more HEROic leader. It can be someone at work, such as another manager, an assistant, or a friend in a different department. However, the best choice is probably someone outside of the organization who can be entirely objective about your work situations. Whoever you choose, it must be someone you respect and trust to give you helpful feedback. You must also be willing to receive feedback and make changes based on the truth partner's suggestions. The idea is to tell your truth partner about HEROic leadership, your goals, and what you are trying to accomplish. For example, you may feel you are too optimistic, and you are working to cultivate a more realistic approach to issues. Your truth partner must be comfortable speaking up and telling you when you are letting your optimism get the better of you.

Your truth partner is like a mirror showing an accurate reflection of yourself, not just your Instagram image. Without this kind of valuable, solidly objective feedback from your truth partner, your biases can skew your self-evaluation and growth. One of the reasons clients seek me out is for me to become their truth partner. They find it difficult to step outside of themselves and see their progress. I tell it like it is and ask the hard, inescapable questions they need to answer to face their truth and keep moving forward. I've been a secret weapon for many managers who want to make a splash and have a winning team at their firm.

Being on board with the HEROic leadership model and working towards increasing or decreasing competencies in the right direction is taking an incredible step forward in your leadership development. However, it is just as valuable for any manager to see where their team members fall on the HERO scale as well.

How HEROic is Your Team?

Chapter 9

How HEROic is Your Team?

Imagine what it would be like if everyone on your team operated with their optimal level of Hope, Efficacy, Resilience, and Optimism. Pretty nice, right?

However, we are all human and trying to work towards becoming our best selves. Chances are that you do not have a team where everyone is HEROic in every way. It's comforting to know that as the team leader, you can influence your team's level of HERO. First, though, you must understand where the team's deficiencies lie.

Recognizing Hope in Your Team

Now that you have learned a bit about the four competencies, you are equipped to recognize them in others. Examine your team as a whole. Are they hopeful? Or hopeless? Efficacious or codependent? Resilient or fragile? Optimistic or pessimistic?

I once worked with a manager on a high-H team who we'll call Kay. The level of hope on Kay's team was so high it was detrimental. Kay knew this right away because she quickly felt like the only one working on the team with her hope in balance. Kay was trying to achieve the attainable goal while the rest of the team and even the CEO had super high-H and grand ideas to pull the company out of its financial hole. The CEO had even declared, "There will be no layoffs," even though stock prices had dropped from $250 to $40 a share and the company had not hit its quota in multiple quarters. However, the CEO was so hopeful that nobody challenged him. It was very stressful for Kay to stand by and watch things unfold. "It was like waiting to see a car wreck happen," she said. The experience was so stressful it eventually drove her out of the company. Had Kay shared the super high-H of her teammates, she may have been there with her fellow employees as they watched the company go under. Instead, she was at another organization, advancing her career.

On the flip side, I've also seen the occasion when the team leader and manager are low-H. In this dynamic, there is a lot of talk and little action. Two low-H people can spend lots of time considering scenarios and fail to develop a good plan because they are too alike. A healthy mix of hope levels between a manager and their team makes for the best decisions and contingency plans. Look for it. As a manager, you can always work to correct any imbalance you notice.

Recognizing Efficacy in Your Team

As managers, we all want to have a high-E team. Will all be well if both the team and the leader have high-E? Not exactly.

I once worked with a manager in the healthcare industry who was very high-E. We'll call her Jill. She was very productive for the company, but she would not do anything that compromised care or access to care. Because of that, her values sometimes clashed with the organization. When the company wanted to sell a pharmaceutical at a price that would make the drug inaccessible to the average person, Jill dug in her heels. She was no longer on board with the commercial implications of the new drug. Despite her feelings and problems with her superiors, Jill's team excelled because the team was collectively very high-E and also motivated by the commercial potential of the drug. Jill, however, ended up moving on from the company.

High-E managers with a high-E team can also fall prey to stifling innovation in favor of quick results. Doing so can lead to shortcuts, quick fixes, and a less-than-ideal outcome. It can also lead to dissatisfied team members who feel unappreciated and unheard.

On the other hand, low-E managers with low-E teams are akin to the blind leading the blind. Both sides need to improve their skills and confidence. Working within such an environment can be very discouraging for both sides. If you identify as a low-E manager and realize you have a low-E team, try your best to seek some proper coaching for the team to raise their "E." (See Chapter 10 for suggestions)

Meanwhile, high-E managers with low-E teams have lots of challenges ahead of them. You will immediately recognize if you are a high-E with a low-E team by your level of frustration. There is help for your team, but the road will probably be longer than you think. Interventions will be key. Be patient and hang in there! You are efficacious and given enough time, you can affect change!

You may feel uneasy if you're a low-E manager with a high-E team. Imposter syndrome sets in. Your team is so competent that you may wonder if you are qualified to lead them. The good news is that you can always grow in your leadership skills. There are plenty of resources available to do it. (See Chapter 10)

Recognizing Resilience in Your Team

High-R is a good thing. But a manager with super high-R will completely stress out a team with low-R. The team may have urgent questions and concerns that the manager might ignore or deflect. If you identify yourself as high-R and know your team to be low-R, be sensitive to the needs of those around you. They may need you to be responsive and explanatory in your leadership. Schedule enough time for the team to complete work and resist the urge to procrastinate. If you remember that your team works differently than you, your dynamic can still thrive, even if you and your team are on the extreme ends of the "R" spectrum.

The high-R team with the high-R manager is doubly blessed. The team can weather whatever comes their way. They will often see eye-to-eye on what is happening and what to do about it. Carry on and thrive!

On the other hand, the "double low-R" situation can be very messy. I have found that it's common for Millennial leaders or even Generation X leaders to have low-R. It is often true for managers who have not had to lead their team through periods of adversity or economic uncertainty, like the mortgage crisis of 2008. We build our resilience through our triumph over negative experiences. If leaders do not experience hardship and a challenge of their spirit and leadership skills, they may never build resilience. Leaders who cannot call upon their personal or professional stores of the resource (like Joel in Chapter 6) may be unable to set a good example for their team. They also may not perform well in a crisis. If you know that both you and your team are low-R, the best thing you can do is prepare for failure. If and when a disaster hits, you will be able to lead your team through it with resilience, even if your team flounders.

A low-R manager with a high-R team will be surprised to see how well their team handles a crisis. It's a time when the team leader can genuinely learn from their team. However, it also puts a leader at a disadvantage when implementing solutions. Again, preparation is essential for any low-R manager who will undoubtedly face a test of resilience at some point.

Recognizing Optimism in Your Team

If your optimism is mid to high-R, you know you have a low-O team if you need help motivating them. If your team seems unengaged or you experience unusually high turnover, it may be because low-O is running rampant through the ranks. In this case, your job is to figure out something that fires up the team. What gets them excited and makes them see the potential for the future? Is it their future and advancement in the company? Or a particular challenge? Sometimes a manager can fight low team-O by being proactive about assignments. Check your frustration at the door and let your team know that you trust them, but they need to look ahead to the future and plan accordingly. Low-O people often need more specific direction.

When the manager is high-O and so is the team, be wary of too many "yes" people in the mix. Too much affirmation can create an unhealthy ecosystem for any leader, but especially when they are already too high-O. They will likely make unrealistic plans if everyone around them flippantly affirms ideas instead of identifying their weaknesses and guarding against vulnerabilities. Ideally, your team should challenge you. They should be able to have a difficult conversation with you to arrive at the best possible solution.

Another problem with the high-O leader and the high-O team is that they may be too much alike. They don't want to challenge each other because neither side wants conflict nor hurt feelings. Both sides are afraid to say, "No, it's just not possible to get it all done this year."

The high-O manager with the low-O team must have the stamina to succeed. The manager must continually motivate their team to a place where they can accept more optimism. Coaching or consulting interventions can be very effective for the high-O, low-O dynamic.

On the other hand, the low-O manager with a high-O team will feel pushed and uncomfortable. The manager will balk at the team's positive ideas and could even hold the team back. If this sounds like your situation, know that working on your optimism could do your team some good.

Leader PsyCap and the Corporate Culture

Are you sensing a theme when it comes to managers and their teams? With HERO competencies, it's not good for a manager to be the same as everyone else on the team. The key to a well-balanced dynamic between manager and team is diversity.

In today's workplace, the term "diversity" refers to the mix of racial, ethnic, and gender populations within a work environment. However, I'm using it differently. Diversity can also include the opportunity for team members with varying degrees of HERO competencies to share their diverse ideas and experiences to facilitate effective decision-making. As mentioned previously, if all of your team is high-O or low-R (or too much of any good thing), your productivity can suffer. There may be tunnel vision about goals. The lack of diversity of opinions can take its toll. On the other hand, a team culture of sharing ideas and respecting the opinion of others can help your team grow in all four HERO competencies.

In my dissertation, I asserted that organizations should consider training leaders on positive leadership behaviors since transformational leadership, or more supportive, caring leadership behaviors are associated with better team outcomes (Avey, Hughes, & Norman, 2008) (Wang, Sui, Wang, & & Wu, 2014) Organizations can then train leaders on leadership skills as well as training all employees to improve their psychological capital. (Boone, 2020) Of course, whether or not an organization embraces PsyCap has much to do with the corporate culture. And whether or not you, as a people manager, can impact your team with HEROic leadership is also influenced by your corporate culture.

I identified the effect of an organization's culture as another implication of my research. Organizational culture is essential for determining a team leader's impact and ability to create a HEROic team. A leader may be well-balanced in the four HERO competencies. However, they may be unable to grow these competencies on an individual level if they are in an unsupportive culture. Or they may become discouraged and unable to transfer valuable PsyCap concepts to the team. In this way, a toxic work environment can keep a solid, HEROic leader from positively impacting and shaping their team.

If you are in such an organization, you have a tough job. You must make strides to create a positive environment within your team while you slowly work towards a fundamental culture shift in the organization. Only then will you be able to be your true, HEROic self at work and develop HEROic team members.

Changing the corporate culture is a daunting task that may seem impossible. However, it can happen if leaders are allowed to be authentic. To successfully tweak company culture with HEROic leadership, leaders must challenge company norms. If that's not possible, they must start incrementally at the individual report and aggregate team levels. Research from Luthans, Avey, Chen, Avolio, and Norman has shown that leaders can impact direct reports. It all depends on how they show up daily and engage their team. Leaders must be confident to challenge the organizational status quo to force a cultural shift. They must shake up the organization so the people who do not align with the emerging culture can be shaken out!

Leader's PsyCap and the Team

My inspiration for writing this book sprang from my completed Ph.D. dissertation in organizational leadership. There have been many researchers before me, including those whose work I have cited in this book, who have shown that raising your level of PsyCap competencies on an individual level (in other words, becoming more HEROic on the job) leads to positive changes and greater job satisfaction and performance. In my dissertation, I examined this phenomenon on a different level. I wanted to explore if a leader's level of PsyCap affects their team, especially in organizational citizenship behaviors and job performance.

I had three hypotheses for my research:

1. **There will be a negative relationship between a leader with low psychological capital (HERO) and team desirable organizational citizenship behaviors.** (Boone, 2020) By testing this hypothesis, I wanted to establish a baseline for my study and use the leader's level of psychological capital as a variable to test group relationships. Several studies from Luthans, Avery, Youssef, and Avolio found that a relationship exists between developing psychological capital in leaders using human resources development interventions (Luthans et al., 2010).

2. **A leader with high psychological capital will positively affect job performance.** (Boone, 2020) The purpose of this hypothesis was to establish that leaders with lower levels of psychological capital have a negative relationship with group organizational citizenship behaviors. Since a leader's level of psychological capital affects the individual's psychological capital, I believed there would also be a group effect. I hypothesized that a leader's level of PsyCap would alter how the teams define OCBs and contribute to team effectiveness (Podsakoff & Mackenzie, 1983).

3. **A leader with high psychological capital will positively affect team job performance.** (Boone, 2020) This hypothesis seemed plausible since researchers had found that a follower's identification with their leader influences job performance. Also,

there are benefits to training employees to develop their PsyCap, which in turn can promote improved job performance (Tüzün, Çetin, & Basim, 2018). Throughout my literature review, I found empirical relationships between organizational performance and OCBs. (Podsakoff & Mackenzie, 1983). On a personal level, in my management coaching, I regularly see PsyCap influence job performance at the individual level, as research proves. (Luthans et al., 2010).

Given our discussion about PsyCap, these three hypotheses may appear easy to prove, especially since other researchers before me have verified similar theories. (Chen, 2015) For my dissertation, I dutifully collected my survey results from the participants, calculated the results, and was thoroughly shocked by what I found. I was unable to prove any of the three hypotheses correct! However, the results do not mean that my hypotheses were incorrect. There are other reasons for the outcome.

Research Explained

All research studies have some limitations. You are invited to read the entire 118 pages of my dissertation to cross-examine my methodologies, measurements, my multilevel regression analysis, summaries, and comparisons and contrasts to prior research. However, the main limitation of this study was my sample size. I completed my research in 2020, the year of COVID-19, and a difficult time capturing the attention and participation of businesspeople. I managed to attain a sample of 89 participants, from entry-level to C-suite, and I gave them a survey where they could self-report their level of PsyCap. I used the PCQ-12 and another tool to measure their OCB. My survey categorized the sample into leaders and followers, and I ended up with a very minimal sample of only 17 qualified leaders for the study.

My smaller sample size was consistent with recommendations (Hox, 2010) but made it difficult to find significant associations among the variables. Also, the overall sample was still smaller than usual for multilevel studies, which looked at how PsyCap in the leader affected their teams. The average number of groups included in prior multilevel models was about 50 (Maas & Hox, 2005).

The researcher I was emulating, Christopher Chen, had also done his study across one organization where mine had pulled from various organizations. Chen gathered data at different periods, while mine was a single collection of data. There is always a possibility of response bias too. A person completing the survey may not answer honestly because they are concerned about confidentiality, how their answers will fare in the study, or they are just having a bad day. Chen used a sample of 379 participants (compared to my 89), leaving plenty of room to dilute the effect of response bias.

Another consideration is that Chen's sample was from a Taiwanese business, and mine was from corporate America. Though my findings differed from Chen (2015), my results were consistent with those of Ratzlaff (2017), who also failed to prove that a leader's psychological capital was associated with team aggregate psychological capital. Similarly, Ratzlaff used a smaller sample from a single American organization. However, Ratzlaff, like many researchers before him, did find that individual psychological capital was associated with individual work engagement levels. In other words, an individual with higher levels of PsyCap reported more work engagement. Therefore, it is possible that a leader's psychological capital is only associated with employee psychological capital under certain conditions and has little to do with the methodological differences that underlie these differing findings. The conditions that may affect employee PsyCap may range from organizational culture or leadership to the broader culture one lives in. (Boone, 2020)

Even though I failed to prove my hypotheses about leadership PsyCap affecting their team through my study, my work does reveal implications for practice that organizations and individual leaders should consider. One of my biggest takeaways was the following:

Businesses should focus on increasing individual psychological capital in their workers. There is still substantial literature showing that individual psychological capital is associated with job performance (Luthans, Avolio, et al., 2007). Research shows that it may be faster and more cost-effective to train leaders to increase their PsyCap to improve followers' psychological capital, OCB, and job performance. Improving all psychological capital at work has several benefits for employees (Avey, Luthans, & Mhatre,

2011) (Rego et al., 2012) (Euwema, et al., 2007) and the organization (e.g., organizational commitment; Larson & Luthans, 2007). Therefore, organizations should continue implementing, training, and fostering a corporate culture that improves psychological capital. (Boone, 2020)

Assessing HERO in Your Team

If you are on board with building a more HEROic team, the first step is understanding your team's level of HERO. And that calls for an assessment.

The simplest way to determine the amount of HERO in your team is by asking them to take an assessment similar to the one you took (See Appendix 3). After your team has taken the assessment, tabulate the results for each individual and determine whether they are low, medium, or high in each of the different competencies. Then determine your team's overall "super score" for each competency. Record one score (L-M-or H) in the last row of the chart for each competency (H-E-R-O) based on the frequency of the answers you received from the individual assessments. Use the team score sheet (Appendix 4) to determine which competencies your team needs to develop further.

Now reference **Appendix** 5, the **HEROic Leadership Team Development Plan.** In each column, indicate by encircling the corresponding letter to indicate your level of each HEROic dimension, both for you as a leader and for the team.

Do the results surprise you? Or were they what you expected? Now that you understand where you and your team stand on the HEROic scale, you can use the information to become a better leader and build a better team. Bookmark the Development Plan because you will be completing it in the next chapter.

In the meantime, let's look at the way organizations are turning to experts to help them engage their team leaders and teams to introduce PsyCap and HERO into their ecosystems. To do so involves specific exercises and activities that are often unexpected, strategic, and impactful. In other words, an intervention!

DEVELOPING HERO IN YOUR TEAM

Chapter 10

Developing HERO in your Team

They say knowledge is power. So now that you understand HERO, your level of it and your team's level too, the secret is out. You are empowered with exclusive knowledge to go forth and create an even stronger team with powerful HERO competencies.

We know that we can develop all of the HERO competencies. However, it takes a new way of thinking-- a mindset shift from the negative to the positive. We also know we can raise low levels of any competency to medium or even high levels with an impactful initiative. Often this initiative comes in the way of a powerful interjection of positive psychology into the workplace. In other words, an intervention.

Effectiveness of Interventions

When you hear the word "intervention," you may think of a person with a substance abuse problem being surprised by a visit from their loved ones, followed by a serious talk about how the abuser needs to change their life. The methods are different in a workplace intervention, but both types of interventions strive for the same result: positive change. An intervention in positive psychology is known as a Positive Psychology Intervention (PPI). It is an effective tool for raising HEROES in the workplace.

One of the earliest PPIs was developed by Michael W. Fordyce, a researcher in the field of empirical happiness measurement. In 1977 he successfully tested a theory to raise the happiness of community college students by modifying their behaviors with positive psychology. (Fordyce, 1977)

Other researchers built on his work by examining the effectiveness of positive psychology interventions. In 2005, a group of psychologists tested different psychological interventions to raise positive feelings, behaviors, and cognitions. (Seligman, Steen, Park, & Peterson, 2005) They examined specific types of positive psychology interventions such as writing letters of gratitude, visiting others, thinking about three good things from each day, writing stories of best personal strengths and re-reading them, and using signature strengths inventories and choosing one to build upon in the coming week. Their work concluded that positive interventions could one day create a legacy of positive psychology. (Seligman, Steen, Park, & Peterson, 2005) Later, researchers Nancy Sin and Sonja Lyubomir performed a famous meta-analysis of 51 PPI interventions on 4,266 individuals. Their work concluded that PPIs significantly increase well-being and decrease depressive symptoms. (Sin & Lyubomirsky, 2009)

Studies on PPIs in the workplace continued. One study concentrated on building up HERO competencies like optimism and efficacy. The study employed two different intervention groups. The first focused on positive aspects in the workplace and the proliferation of gratitude and challenged team members to notice and process good things about their coworkers and environment. The PPI for the second intervention group helped team members deal with setbacks and explore different ways of coping with adversity and improving problem-solving. The ten-week study was conducted in Sweden.

While both training sessions were successful, the first intervention group, which focused on the positivity of the workplace, had the most dramatic results. The research proved it was possible to raise PsyCap with a PPI, and the effects of the PPI remained in place six months after the intervention. (Harty, Gustafsson, Bjorkdahl, & Moller, 2016) When asked how the training had changed them at work, all but one of the 29 respondents said they had noticed a positive change in their attitude at work. Other participants noted an increased understanding, tolerance, and confidence in themselves. Many also reported feeling more engaged and positive about work and colleagues. (Harty, Gustafsson, Bjorkdahl, & Moller, 2016)

In general, researchers believe PPIs are effective, but results vary. (White, Uttl, & Holder, 2019) Many studies on positive psychology have concluded that the most dramatic results effects occur in subjects who need PPIs the most. In other words, the people who entered the study with low levels of self-enhancement benefited more from the intervention than those who came to it with an already high amount of HERO. (Harty, Gustafsson, Bjorkdahl, & Moller, 2016). However, even people on the higher end of the HERO scale can benefit from a well-run PPI and the opportunities it presents.

One day I was leading a training session as an outside consultant with the lower management and the C-Suite of a large organization. When it was time to split into breakout groups, we divided the C-Suite into one group and the other lower management team into several others. As I sat observing the dynamics of the upper management group and looking around the circle of chairs, I recalled that this particular group of professionals was very HEROic and high in all four competencies. They were hopeful about what they could accomplish, very confident in their space, optimistic, and quite resilient since their organization had recently survived a great deal of turbulence, including a change in ownership.

The C-team began their discussion on the training principles, as was their assignment for the breakout group. Then, as they started to discuss goal-setting, they comfortably transitioned into a productive, high-level strategic discussion about their company right before my eyes. They were brainstorming and getting so much done that when the allotted time was up, I regretted interrupting them to rejoin the rest of the group for the conclusion of the training. I immediately assumed that the C-suite had taken advantage of their time together to make progress on previous discussions. I felt like their entire interaction had been the continuation of a previous meeting. Out of curiosity, I asked a nearby VP how often the team gathers to have such discussions.

"Never," he answered, to my amazement. "This session showed us we need to make time for more discussions like that."

Even though the C-team was undisputedly HEROic, it took an intervention to get them to a higher level. The intervention taught them that when they were relieved of direct reports and could focus on strategy, the results could be phenomenal. Their next step was to adjust their schedules to include time for more strategic sessions. Since they were all high-E leaders, that's surely what they did!

In this example, the PPI helped the HEROic senior leaders in a completely unexpected way. Interventions do more than educate; they inspire, motivate, and allow employees to focus in different directions.

How to Secure A PPI Intervention

There are two ways to bring a PPI into your workplace—through internal team development or an outside consultant. In my career, I have delivered PPIs as part of both types of teams.

As a rising professional in human resources, I delivered staff training to my coworkers. As a current management consultant, I lead complex organizations in realigning their goals and bringing positive psychology into the workplace with impressive results. The method you choose for your intervention should depend on many factors, including your corporate needs, your access to resources, and your company culture.

Internal Team Development

Internal team development is precisely what it sounds like. Someone from inside the organization leads the team in a developmental intervention. Internal team development is usually led by the human resources department or, in a larger organization, a development team. The team's familiarity with the person delivering the training can help or hinder the program's results, depending upon the organizational culture. Just as children don't always like to listen to their parents, sometimes people learn better from outside experts who have no history with the company or its employees.

Internal interventions may vary in complexity. The simplest intervention would be for a manager to ask the team to read a book from an organizational development expert (like this one!) and hold a group discussion about the book and how to apply the principles in the workplace. Another option is to conduct in-house training from a fully developed, "canned" program, including do-it-yourself workshop outlines, workbooks, or ready-made resources.

Keeping the training in-house is the most economical way to bring training into the organization. However, results can vary widely depending on the program itself and the trainer's experience and comfort level in delivering the material.

Regardless of who delivers an internal training program, the management team must unequivocally support the effort. It's also critical that both the trainer and the management agree on the program's goals and how to evaluate the success of the program. The only way to deem internal training successful is if clear goals are set ahead of time and then evaluated to see if the organization reached those goals.

External Consulting Programs

Bringing in a partner or firm to help with a PPI intervention brings many advantages. Outside leadership or management development firms employ organizational experts, psychologists, and leadership experts to assist your company in becoming a stronger, more productive team. The program they deliver should address your organization's needs.

The PPI can be as in-depth or as elementary as needed. Most firms offer varying levels of service, based on your goals. The PPI can be an existing program delivered over a day, a half day, or a more in-depth program delivered over a series of sessions.

The depth of the PPI may vary, depending on the organization's resources. Consulting firms can build a program specifically for your organization if the organization is willing to make an investment. They typically begin with a meeting to discuss your concerns and do a complete evaluation of your team members' skills, personalities, strengths, and weaknesses. Consultants may administer written assessments, followed by in-depth personal interviews with employees. The consultant may administer a proprietary written assessment or use one of the industry's gold standard versions, such as Meyers-Briggs, Clifton Strengths, etc.

You can count on high-quality, proven methods. Leadership firms build their reputation on their successful case studies. If their methods don't work, they have no following and are soon forced out of the very competitive leadership development market. Still, look at online reviews and ask trusted sources for recommendations and referrals to a good consultant or consulting firm.

Finding the Right Expert

Leadership development experts come in all shapes and sizes. There are huge, established development firms; there are also many entrepreneurs who have built successful leadership coaching practices with an impressive track record of success.

While it's more economical for smaller firms to hire a smaller consultancy or an entrepreneur coach, remember that your goal should be to find the right-sized and affordable consultant for your organization, but also one who will deliver a program that will positively impact the quality of your workplace. In many cases, you get what you pay for when it comes to development programs. Low fees may translate to low quality programs.

Regardless of whether you are vetting individual consultants or firms, there will be questions to ask before bringing anyone aboard. Here are a few questions to use as a starting point if you want to engage a consultant who can help your team be more HEROic.

Are you familiar with the HERO competencies?

Have you helped employees at other organizations increase their HERO competencies?

What relationship do your coaching methods have with positive psychology?

Could you help us increase HERO with your methodology?

What would be your process for working with an organization like ours?

How do you know when your program has been successful?

What goals do you typically work on with your other organizations?

Be sure whoever you hire is clear on upper management's expectations and plans to measure the success of the program. Clear expectations are critical for a smooth working relationship between your consultant and your organization.

Whether you stay in-house for your leadership development or hire an outside expert, understanding your HERO level and your team's gives you a great foundation. Besides providing valuable information about your team, you can use the assessment results from this book to help you plan and make better decisions with anyone your organization hires to raise your HEROic leadership. Any work you do assessing HERO for you and your team will pay off when it's time to plan your development program.

The HERO Leadership Team Development Plan Sheet

It's time to return to Appendix 5, the HERO Leadership Team Development Plan Sheet. On it, you can analyze the results of your HERO assessment and the one for your team. What do the results say about you as a leader and how you relate to your team? If you were speaking to a consultant right now, how would you describe your team's strengths and weaknesses (development areas)? Fill in Part II of the Development Plan Sheet with your thoughts.

The final part of the Development Plan Sheet is for creating team goals, expected outcomes, and desired action items for the team. Complete Part III to the best of your ability. Then, share it with the three most interested parties in seeing this information.

Top Management. Any intervention must be approved from the top. Present the findings of the HERO assessments and use the material in this book to support the need for a PPI in your organization. Ensure that top management understands and supports the PPI and also agrees on the goals of the intervention and how it will be evaluated for effectiveness.

The Internal Development Team. The Development Plan Sheet is beneficial for organizations planning to create an in-house PPI. The information on the development sheet can narrow the focus of the PPI so the internal team can create and deliver a relevant, effective program.

Outside Consultants. The sheet can also be helpful when you are hiring an outside consultant to deliver a PPI at your organization. Prepare the sheet in advance and share it with the experts so they have a quick snapshot of your team's HERO ecosystem. The information will give them a starting point to begin planning their PPI and can even help them optimize their program delivery.

The Future of HEROic Leadership

You have now examined the idea of HEROic leadership from all angles. You have assessed yourself and your team. You have a clear vision of what HERO can achieve within your organization. It is now up to you to let your organization in on the secret of HERO and all it can do for its leaders and teams.

Hope, Efficacy, Resilience, and Optimism are in short supply in our world now, but even more so in the workplace. Although the study of positive psychology and PsyCap has been around for decades, it has yet to get the attention it deserves. It is one of the reasons I wrote this book. I first heard about HERO as I entered my Ph.D. program. Today, most leadership experts are not routinely addressing HERO in their training, even with all the research backing it up as a valuable tool.

If you bring in an expert to your organization, I encourage you to find one who understands positive psychology, PsyCap, and HERO. For in-house programs, this book can serve as an invaluable resource. It explains the HERO competencies and the science behind them. It also provides a practical assessment for team members and leaders with hints on how to work well given everyone's HERO competency levels.

Now that you know the secret of HERO, my hope is for you to experience a HEROic workplace with HEROic leaders. However, my greatest hope is for you to become the most HEROic leader you can be. The world will look different if it has a bit more HERO in it. I wish you the best in becoming a more HEROic leader and hope you will become part of a movement to create a better workplace and a better world. Start at your organization and take it from there. HERO shouldn't be a secret any longer!

APPENDICES

APPENDIX 1

LEADER HERO ASSESSMENT

Below is the Leader HERO assessment in its entirety. Throughout the book, five questions assessing each of the HERO competencies appeared at the end of each chapter. If you have already completed each of the assessments, turn to Appendix 2 and record your score for each competency. If not, please complete the assessment below.

For each question, choose the number that corresponds most closely with your answer:

Strongly Disagree	Disagree	Somewhat Disagree	Agree	Strongly Agree
1	2	3	4	5

HOPE

1. I feel I am basically successful as a leader of my team.

1	2	3	4	5

2. I have set goals with my team and am motivated to pursue them.

1	2	3	4	5

3. My team meets the goals that are set for them.

1   2   3   4   5

4. As a leader, I believe there are many ways to solve any problem.

1   2   3   4   5

5. My team and I have more than one solution to every problem.

1   2   3   4   5

SELF EFFICACY

1. I feel confident assessing business problems and proposing solutions.

1   2   3   4   5

2. I feel confident in presenting my work area to senior leaders.

1   2   3   4   5

3. I feel confident sharing my thoughts on strategic initiatives.

1   2   3   4   5

4. I feel confident setting goals and objectives in my work area.

1   2   3   4   5

5. I feel confident connecting with internal and external stakeholders for advice when I have a problem.

1   2   3   4   5

RESILIENCE

1. I have trouble moving on after a setback at work.

1   2   3   4   5

2. I'm able to manage difficulties at work.

1   2   3   4   5

3. I can work independently, no matter what happens.

1   2   3   4   5

4. I don't let work stress get to me.

1   2   3   4   5

5. I've experienced difficulties at work before and can therefore get through them.

1   2   3   4   5

OPTIMISM

1. I expect the best to happen at work, even when I don't know what's around the corner.

   1   2   3   4   5

2. If I'm in a position where something can go wrong, I think about it working out instead.

   1   2   3   4   5

3. I'm optimistic about what will happen to me in the future at work.

   1   2   3   4   5

4. Things usually happen the way I want them to in my job.

   1   2   3   4   5

5. I can find the silver lining in almost every situation I encounter at work.

   1   2   3   4   5

APPENDIX 2

HEROic LEADER SCORE SHEET

COMPETENCY	SUM TOTAL OF POINTS FROM ASSESSMENT Add up the numbers from the answers you circled in each of the sections of the HERO assessment. Your number should range from the lowest score of 5 (1 per question) to 25 (5 per question) for each competency.	COMPETENCY LEVEL Indicate L-M-H based on your total score. 20-25 HIGH 12-19 MEDIUM 5 – 11 LOW
Hope		
Efficacy		
Resilience		
Optimism		
SUM TOTAL		

APPENDIX 3

TEAM HERO ASSESSMENT

For each question, choose the number that corresponds most closely with your answer:

Strongly Disagree	Disagree	Somewhat Disagree	Agree	Strongly Agree
1	2	3	4	5

HOPE

1. I feel I am basically successful within my team.

1	2	3	4	5

2. I am motivated to pursue the goals set for my team.

1	2	3	4	5

3. I help my team meet the goals set for them.

1	2	3	4	5

4. I believe there are many ways to solve any problem.

1	2	3	4	5

5. My team and I have more than one solution to every problem.

1   2   3   4   5

SELF EFFICACY

1. I feel confident assessing business problems and proposing solutions to my team.

1   2   3   4   5

2. I feel confident in representing my work to others.

1   2   3   4   5

3. I feel confident contributing to discussions about the team's progress.

1   2   3   4   5

4. I feel confident helping to set targets/goals for myself.

1   2   3   4   5

5. I feel confident connecting with my team and external stakeholders for advice when I have a problem.

1   2   3   4   5

RESILIENCE

1. I have very little trouble moving on after a setback at work.

   1   2   3   4   5

2. I'm able to manage difficulties at work.

   1   2   3   4   5

3. I can work independently, no matter what happens.

   1   2   3   4   5

4. I don't let work stress get to me.

   1   2   3   4   5

5. I've experienced difficulties at work before and can therefore get through them.

   1   2   3   4   5

OPTIMISM

1. I expect the best to happen at work, even when I don't know what's around the corner.

   1   2   3   4   5

2. If I'm in a position where something can go wrong, I think about it working out instead.

1   2   3   4   5

3. I'm optimistic about what will happen to me in the future at work.

1   2   3   4   5

4. Things usually happen the way I want them to with my team.

1   2   3   4   5

5. I can find the silver lining in almost every situation I encounter at work.

1   2   3   4   5

SCORING DIRECTIONS FOR LEADER:

For each team member assessment, add up the numbers from the answers circled in each of the four sections. Numbers should range from the lowest score of 5 (1 per question) to 25 (5 per question) for each competency.

On the Team HERO Score Sheet in Appendix 4, record the competency level (H-M-L) for each team member for each competency.

APPENDIX 4

HEROic TEAM SCORESHEET

In the far-left column, list the names of the team members taking the assessments. Use an additional piece of paper if necessary. Under each HERO column, record whether the corresponding team member is H-M-L in each competency. In the last row, enter the mode (most often occurring) level in each column. This is your team's score for each competency.

TEAM MEMBER NAME	HOPE SCORE	EFFICACY SCORE	RESILIENCE SCORE	OPTIMIS M SCORE
TEAM SCORE (MOST OCCURING) IN EACH COMPETENCY				

APPENDIX 5

HERO LEADERSHIP TEAM DEVELOPMENT PLAN

Leader Name: _____

Department/Team: _____

PART 1: ASSESSMENT RESULTS : Record the results of
the leader and Team HEROic dimension scores.

Leader HEROic Dimensions	Team HEROic Dimensions
Hope: L M H	Hope: L M H
Efficacy: L M H	Efficacy: L M H
Resilience: L M H	Resilience: L M H
Optimism: L M H	Optimism: L M H

PART II: TEAM STRENGTHS AND WEAKNESSES
(Based on HERO levels of leader and team)

KEY TEAM STRENGTHS	KEY DEVELOPMENT AREAS
• XXX	• XXX
• XXX	• XXX
• XXX	• XXX

PART III: DEVELOPMENT ACTIONS (COMPLETE WITH DEVELOPMENT LEADER)

Team Goal	Outcome/ Impact	Action (Behaviors, Experiences, Relationships)
xxx	• xxx • xxx	• xxx • xxx
xxx	• xxx • xxx	• xxx • xxx
xxx	• xxx • xxx	• xxx • xxx

ABOUT THE AUTHOR

Melonie Boone, Ph. D. is a global business psychologist, leadership strategist, positive leader scholar, and serial entrepreneur engaged in helping others reach their full potential in their personal and professional lives.

Using positive psychology as a foundation to coach others to high performance, Dr. Boone has built a dynamic career as a leader and trusted advisor to executives on strategy, operations, P&L management, leadership development, and human resources for organizations from startups to large global companies. She has devoted over 25 years to affecting transformational change in leaders and their organizations and specializes in helping women and people of color navigate the complexities that arise in corporate settings. Her strategies have yielded significant results with individuals and corporations within financial services, technology, manufacturing, pharmaceuticals, consumer products, professional services, family-owned businesses, retail, municipalities, healthcare, education, publishing, restaurants, and more.

Dr. Boone is the creator of a business acceleration framework to launch a business in 60 days. She used the model to successfully launch her many service and retail entrepreneurial efforts, including her management consulting firm focused on leadership development, B Ana Studios; her Business B.I.T.E.S. online micro-lesson platform; Blue Havana Clothing, an upscale boutique; and Blue Havana Cigar Shop.

In 2009, Dr. Boone launched a speaking career and is currently a noted keynote speaker with more than 40 appearances. She is available to speak on topics ranging from transformational leadership to personal branding, business strategy, entrepreneurship, global business operations, safety, social media, positive leadership, and much more.

Dr. Boone serves on the board of Future Cycle Breakers, a nonprofit organization providing underserved communities with Entrepreneurial Business Education to create opportunities for generating wealth. She holds a Ph.D. in organizational leadership from the Chicago School of Professional Psychology, an M.J. from Loyola University Chicago School of Law, an MBA from Florida Metropolitan University, and a B.B.A in Human Resource Management from Loyola University in Chicago. She lives in Chicago with her husband, where they are raising their son and daughter.

To learn more about Melonie, visit
https://melonieboonephd.com

HEROic Leadership References

Chapter 1

Avey, J. B., Luthans, F., & Mhatre, K. H. (2011). Meta-analysis of the impact of positive psychological capital on employee attitudes, behaviors, and performance. *Human Resource Development Quarterly 22(2)*, 127-152.

Avey, J., Hughes, L., & Norman, S. &. (2008). Using positivity, transformational leadership and empowerment to combat employee negativity. *Leadership & Organization Development Journal 29(2)*, 110-126.

Luthans, F. (2012). Psychological capital: Implications for HRD, retrospective analysis, and future directions. *Human Resource Development Quarterly, 23*(1), 1–8. https://doi.org/10.1002/hrdq.21119

Rego, A., Filipa, S., Maques, C., & Cunah, M. P. e. (2012). Authentic leadership promoting employees' psychological capital and creativity. *Journal of Business Research*, *65*(3), 429 -437. https://doi.org/10.1016/J.JBUSRES.2011.10.003

Chapter 2

Abramis, D. J., & Beach, L. (2017). Relationship of job stressors to job performance : linear or an inverted-U ?, (February). https://doi.org/10.2466/pr0.1994.75.1.54 7

Avey, J. B., Luthans, F., & Mhatre, K. H. (2011). Meta-analysis of the impact of positive psychological capital on employee attitudes, behaviors, and performance. *Human Resource Development Quarterly 22(2)*, 127-152.

Chen, S. (2015). The relationship of leader psychological capital and follower psychological capital, job engagement and job performance: a multilevel mediating perspective. *International Journal of Human Resource Management*.

Jogulu, U. D. (2010). Culturally-linked leadership styles. *Leadership & Organization Development Journal*, *31*(8),

705–719. https://doi.org/10.1108/014377310110947
66 Luthans, F., & Youssef-Morgan, C. M. (2017).
Psychological Capital: An Evidence-Based Positive
Approach. *Annu. Rev. Organ. Psychol. Organ.
Behav, 4*, 339–366.

Luthans, F., & Youssef-Morgan, C. (2017). Psychological
Capital: An Evidence-Based Positive Approach. *Annu.
Rev. of Organ. Psych. Organ. Behav*, 339-66.

Chapter 3

American Management Association. (2007). *Leading the Four
Generations at Work.* Amanet.org.

Boitnott, J. (2016, January 27). *Generation Z and the
Workplace: What You Need to Know.* Inc.

Boone, M. M. (2020). *The Impact of Leader Psychological
Capital on Team Outcomes and Behaviors: A Multilevel
Analysis.* Chicago: ProQuest.

Bursch, D. a. (2014). *Managing the Multigenerational
Workplace*. UNC Kenan-Flagler Business School,
Executive Development.

Deloitte. (2016). *The 2016 Deloitte Millennial Survey.* Deloitte .

Elena Comperatore, H. U. (2008). Coping With Different Generations in the Workplace. *Journal of Business & Economics Research*, 15-29.

EY. (2015). *Global Generations: A Global Study on Work-Life Challenges Across Generations* . EY.

Finn, D. a. (2013). *PwC's Next Gen: A Global Generational Study.* PwC.

Jones, L. (2017). Strategies for Retaining a Multigenerational Workforce. *Journal of Business and Financial Affairs* , 6:2.

Manpower Group. (2016). *Millennial Careers: 2020 Vision.* Manpower Group.

Moss, D. (2017). *5 Generations + 7 Values = Endless Opportunities.* Society for Human Resources Management.

Notter, J. (2013). *Conflict and Generations in the Workplace.* Association for Talent Development, Management Blog.

Rodriguez, M. (2015). *Five Strategies for Managing Generational Differences.* bsci21.org.

s. (n.d.).

Schlitzer, V. (2014). *Tough Questions for Millennials and Employers.* Bentley University: Prepared U Project.

Staples, H. (2014). *The Generational Divide: Generational Differences in Psychological Capital.* Theses & Dissertations.

Steinfield, L. (2017, March 25). Attracting and Retaining Talent in a Knowledge-based Economy: Moving beyond Generational Differences to Create a Conducive Work Environment. *ResearchGate.*

Sturt, D. &. (2016, August 16). Generational Differences: When They Matter and When They Don't. *Forbes .*

University, Center for Women and Business at Bentley. (2017). *Multi-Generational Impacts on the Workplace: A Curated Research Report.* C.

Various. (2017). *Multi-Generational Impacts on the Workplace: A Curated Research Report.* Waltham, MA.

Williams, J. (2016). *Trends in the Workplace.* Arcadis.

WorkplaceTrends. (2016, September 6). GenZ & Millennials Collide at Work. *workplacetrends.com.*

Wu, N. e. (2014). *Engaging and Empowering Millennials.* PwC.

Chapter 4

Adams, V.H., Snyder, C. R., Rand, K. L., King, E. A., Sigmon, D. R., & Pulvers, K.M. (in press). Hope in the workplace. In R. Giacolone & C. Jurkiewicz (Eds), Workplace spirituality and organizational performance. New York: Sharp.

Luthans, F., Avolio, B.J., & Avey, J.B. (2014). *Psychological Capital Questionnaire Manual.* Menlo Park, CA: Mind Garden, Inc.

Snyder, C. R., Lapointe, A. B., Crowson, J. J., Jr., & Early, S. (1998). Preferences of high and low hope people for self-referential input. Cognition and Emotion, 12, 807–823.)—From Luthans, et. All Human Resource Dev. Quarterly 21

Chapter 5

Bandura, A. (1997). Self-efficacy: The exercise of control. New York: Freeman.

Gist, M. E., & Mitchell, T. R. (1992). Self-efficacy: A theoretical analysis of its determinants and malleability. Academy of Management Review, 17, 183-211.

Martocchio, J. J., & Judge, T. A. (1997). Relationships between conscientiousness and learning in employee training: Mediating influences of self-deception and self-efficacy. Journal of Applied Psychology, 82, 764-773.

Schaufeli, W.B. and Salanova, M. (2007), "Work engagement: an emerging psychological concept and its implications for organizations", in Gilliland, S.W., Steiner, D.D. and Skarlicki, D.P. (Eds), Research in Social Issues in Management: Managing Social and Ethical Issues in Organizations, Vol. 5, Information Age Publishers, Greenwich, CT, pp. 135-177.

Shelton, S. H. (1990). Developing the construct of general self-efficacy. Psychological Reports, 66, 987-994.

Sherer, M., & Adams, C. H. (1983). Construct validation of the Self-Efficacy Scale. Psychological Reports, 53, 899-902.

Sherer, M., Maddux, J. E., Mercandante, B., Prentice-Dunn, S., Jacobs, B., & Rogers, R. W.(1982). The Self-Efficacy Scale: Construction and validation. Psychological Reports, 51, 663-671.

Judge, T. A., Erez, A., & Bono, J. A. (1998). The power of being positive: The relation between positive self-concept and job performance. Human Performance, 11, 167-187.

<u>Chapter 6</u>

Baker, F. R., & Baker, K. L. (2021). Introducing the skills-based model of personal resilience: Drawing on content and process factors to build resilience in the workplace. Journal of Occupational and Organizational Psychology (2021), 458-481.

Garmezy, N. (1971). Vulnerability research and the issue of primary prevention. American Journal of Orthopsychiatry, 41:101-116.

Hutchinson, A., Stuart, A., & Pretorius, H. (2010). The relationships amongst temperament, character strengths, and resilience. SA Journal Of Industrial Psychology 36(2) , 1-10.

Jordan, J. (2005). Relational resilience in girls. In E. Goldstein, & R. Brooks, Handbook of resilience in children (pp. 91-105). New York, NY: Springer.

Luthans, F. A. (2007). Positive Psychological Capital: Measurement and Relationship with Performance. Personal Psychology Autumn, 60(3).

Luthans, F., & Jensen, S. (2002). Hope: A New Positive Strength for Human Resources Development. Human Resource Development Review , 304-322.

Luthar, S. S., Cicchetti, D., & Becker, B. (2000). The construct of resilience: a critical evaluation and guidelines for future work. Child Dev. May-June 71 (3), 543-62.

Martinez-Marti, M. L. (2016). Character strengths predict resilience over and above positive affect, self-efficacy, optimism, social support, self-esteem, and life satisfaction. Journal of Positive Psychology (12, 2), 110-119.

Masten, A., & Garmezy, N. (1985). Risk, vulnerability, and protective factors in developmental psychopathology. Advances in Child Psychology(8), pp. 1-52.

Masten, A., & Garmezy, N. (1990). Resilience and development: Contributions from the study of children. Development and Psychopathology, 2:425-444.

Moore, A., & Malinowski, P. (2009). Consciousness and Cognition 18(1) . Retrieved from doi.org: https://doi.org/10.1016/j.concog.2008.12.008

Ozbay, F., Johnson, D., Dimoulas, E., Morgan, C., Charney, D., & Southwick, S. (2007, PMID: 20806028; PMCID: PMC2921311). Social support and resilience to stress: From neurobiology to clinical practice. Retrieved from ncbi.nim.nih.gov: https://www.ncbi.nlm.nih.gov/pmc/articles/

Sun Yung, H., & Hyun Yoon, H. (2015). The impact of employees' positive psychological capital on job satisfaction and organizational citizenship behaviors in the hotel. International Journal of Contemporary Hospitality Management 27(6), 1135-1156.

Chapter 7

Andersson, G. (1996). The benefits of optimism: A meta-analytic review of the Life Orientation Test. Personality and Individual Differences, 719-725.

Arakawa, D. G. (2007). Optimistic managers and their influence on productivity and employee engagement in a technology organization: Implications for coaching psychologists. International Coaching Psychology Review 2(1) , 78-79.

Avey, J. B., Luthans, F., & Mhatre, K. H. (2011). Meta-analysis of the impact of positive psychological capital on employee attitudes, behaviors, and performance. Human Resource Development Quarterly 22(2), 127-152.

Avey, J., Hughes, L., & Norman, S. &. (2008). Using positivity, transformational leadership and empowerment to combat employee negativity. Leadership & Organization Development Journal 29(2), 110-126.

Brydon, L., Walker, C., Wawrzyniak, A. J., Chart, H., & Steptoe, A. (2009). Dispositional optimism and stress-induced changes in immunity and negative mood. Elsevier.

Frost, S. (2021). Optimism at Work: Developing and Validating Scales to Measure Workplace Optimism. Keene, New Hampshire: AURA- Antioch University Repository and Archive.

Gibson, B. &. (2004). Optimism, Pessimism, and Gambling: The Downside of Optimism. Society for Personality and Social Psychology.

Ingersoll, L., Alexander, S. C., Ladwig, S., Anderson, W., Norton, S. A., & Gramling, R. (2019). The contagion of optimism: The relationship between patient optimism and palliative care clinician overestimation of survival among hospitalized patients with advanced cancer. Psycho-Oncology 28(6), 1286-1292.

Ironson, G. M., & Hayward, H. B. (2008). Do Positive Psychosocial Factors Predict Disease Progression in HIV-1? A Review of the Evidence. Psychosomatic Medicine .

Kun, A., & Gadanecz, P. (2022). Workplace happiness, well-being and their relationship with psychological capital: A study of Hungarian teachers. Current Psychology (41), 185-199.

Luthans F., Y. C. (2007). Psychological Capitol. Oxford University Press.

Luthans, F. A. (2007). Positive Psychological Capital: Measurement and Relationship with Performance. Personal Psychology Autumn, 60(3).

Rasmussen, H., & Wrosch, C. S. (2006). Self-Regulation Processes and Health: the Importance of Optimism and Goal Adjustment. Journal of Personality 74(6), 1721-1748.

Schier, M., & Carver, C. (1985). Optimism, coping, and health: Assessment and implications of generalized outcome expectancies. Health Psychology, 219-247.

Schofield, P. &. (2004). Optimism and survival in lung carcinoma patients. ASC Journals 100(6), 1276-1282.

Selig, M. &. (1986). Explanatory style as a predictor of productivity and quitting among life insurance sales agents . Journal of Personality and Social Psychology 50(4), 832-838.

Smith, T. W., & MacKenzie, J. (2006). Personality and Risk of Physical Illness. Annual Review of Clinical Psychology, 435-467.

Steptoe, A., Wright, C., Kunz-Ebrecht, S. R., & Iliffe, S. (2010). Dispositional optimism and health behavior in community-dwelling older people: Associations with healthy ageing. British Journal of Health Psychology, 71-84.

Youssef, C. &. (2007b). Positive Organizational Behavior in the Workplace The Impact of Hope, Optimism, and Resilience. Journal of Management 33 (5), 774-800.

Chapter 8

Kun, A., & Gadanecz, P. (2022). Workplace happiness, well-being and their relationship with psychological capital: A study of Hungarian teachers. *Current Psychology (41)*, 185-199.

Lowney, C. (2011). *The Third Theme of Heroic Leadership: Heroism*. Retrieved from https://www.youtube.com/user/mentorsgallery: https://www.youtube.com/watch?v=CIhfUSzi0po&ab_channel=mentorsgallery

Lowney, C. (n.d.). *Magis-Driven Heroic Leadership is a Daily Personal Pursuit*. Retrieved from Ignationspirtuality.com : https://www.ignatianspirituality.com/ignatian-voices/21st-century-ignatian-voices/magis-driven-heroic-leadership-is-a-daily-personal-pursuit/

Myatt, M. (2012, February 28). *The Problem with Heroic Leaders*. Retrieved from forbes.com: https://www.forbes.com/sites/mikemyatt/2012/02/28/the-problem-with-heroic-leaders/?sh=1501b5275320

Chapter 9

Chen, S.-L. (2015). The relationship of leader psychological capital and follower psychological capital, job engagement and job performance: A multilevel mediating perspective. The International Journal of Human Resource Management, 26(18), 2349–2365.

Boone, M. M. (2020). *The Impact of Leader Psychological Capital on Team Outcomes and Behaviors: A Multilevel Analysis*. Chicago, IL : SAGE.

Euwema, M. C., Wendt, H., & van Emmerik, H. (2007). Leadership styles and group organizational citizenship behavior across cultures. *Journal of Organizational*

Behavior, 28(8), 1035–1057.
https://doi.org/10.1002/job.496

Lam, S. S. K., Hui, C., & Law, K. S. (1999). Organizational
Citizenship Behavior: Comparing Perspectives of
Supervisors and Subordinates Across Four International
Samples. *Journal of Applied Psychology* (Vol. 84).
Retrieved from
https://search-proquestcom.tcsedsystem.idm.oclc.org/d
ocview/614348369/fulltextPDF/2763732AF22A4536P
Q/1? accountid=34120

Larson, M., & Luthans, F. (2007). Potential Added Value of
Psychological Capital in Predicting
Work Attitudes. *Journal of Leadership &*
Organizational Studies, 13(1), 45–62.
https://doi.org/10.1177/10717919070130010701

Luthans, F., Avey, J. B., Avolio, B. J., & Peterson, S. J. (2010).
The Development and Resulting
Performance Impact of Positive Psychological Capital.
Human Resource Development
Quarterly, 21(1), 41–67.
https://doi.org/10.1002/hrdq.20034

Podsakoff, P. M., & Mackenzie, S. B. (1983). Impact of
Organizational Citizenship Behavior on Organizational
Performance: A Review and Suggestions for Future
Research. *Bateman & Organ Brief & Motowidlo, 10*(2),
133–15. Retrieved from
https://www-tandfonlinecom.tcsedsystem.idm.oclc.org/
doi/pdf/10.1207/s15327043hup1002_5?needAccess=tr

Ratzlaff, J. (2017). *Psychological Capital and Employee
Engagement as a Predictor of PatientCare Outcomes.*
Retrieved from
https://search-proquestcom.tcsedsystem.idm.oclc.org/p
qdtglobal/docview/1954047257/17438A14525A4599P
Q/2?accountid=34120

Rego, A., Filipa, S., Maques, C., & Cunah, M. P. e. (2012).
Authentic leadership promoting employees'
psychological capital and creativity. *Journal of Business
Research, 65*(3), 429–
437.
https://doi.org/10.1016/J.JBUSRES.2011.10.003

Tüzün, I. K., Çetin, F., & Basim, H. N. (2018). International
Journal of Productivity and Performance Management
Improving job performance through identification and
psychological capital. *International Journal of*

Productivity and Performance Management, 67(1), 155–170. Retrieved from https://doi.org/10.1108/IJPPM-03-2016-0060

Wang, H., Sui, Y., Wang, D., & & Wu, Y. (2014). Impact of authentic leadership on performance: Role of followers' positive psychological capital and relational processes. *Journal of Organizational Behavior*, 35(1) 5-21. Retrieved from https://doi.org/10.1002/job.1850

Chapter 10

Fordyce, M. (1977). Development of a program to increase personal happiness . *APA PsycNet*, 24(6), 511-521.

Harty, B., Gustafsson, J.-A., Bjorkdahl, A., & Moller, A. (2016). *Group intervention: A way to improve working teams' positive psychological capital.* Netherlands: IOS Press.

Seligman, M., Steen, T., Park, N., & Peterson, C. (2005). Positive Psychology Progress: Empirical Validation of Interventions. *American Psychologist*, 60 (5) 410-421.

Sin, N. L., & Lyubomirsky, S. (2009). Enhancing well-being and alleviating depressive symptoms with positive psychology interventions: a practice-friendly meta-analysis. *Journal of Clinical Psychology*, 467-487.

White, C. A., Uttl, B., & Holder, M. D. (2019). *Meta-analyses of positive psychology interventions: The effects are much smaller than previously reported.* Austria: PLoS ONE.

INDEX